General editor
Peter
Herriot

New
Essential
Psychology

Applying
Psychology
in
Organizations

ALREADY PUBLISHED IN THIS SERIES

Social Interaction and its Management
Judy Gahagan

Instinct, Environment and Behaviour
S.E.G. Lea

Selves in Relation
An introduction to psychotherapy and groups
Keith Oatley

Individual Differences
Theories and applications
Vivian Shackleton and Clive Fletcher

Cognitive Development and Education
Johanna Turner

Learning Theory and Behaviour Modification
Stephen Walker

FORTHCOMING TITLES IN THIS SERIES

Information and Human Performance
Paul J. Barber and David Legge

Physiological Psychology
Theory and applications
John Blundell

Personality Theory and Clinical Practice
Peter Fonagy and Anna Higgit

Cognitive Psychology
Judith Greene

Experimental Design and Statistics
Second edition
Steve Miller

Multivariate Design and Statistics
Steve Miller

Lifespan Development
Concepts, theories and interventions
Léonie Sugarman

Cognitive Social Psychology and Social Policy
Kerry Thomas

Frank Blackler Sylvia Shimmin

Applying Psychology in Organizations

Methuen

London and New York

*First published in 1984 by
Methuen & Co. Ltd
11 New Fetter Lane, London EC4P 4EE*

*Published in the USA by
Methuen & Co.
in association with Methuen, Inc.
733 Third Avenue, New York, NY 10017*

© *1984 Frank Blackler and
Sylvia Shimmin*

*Typeset by Rowland Phototypesetting Ltd
Bury St Edmunds, Suffolk
Printed in Great Britain by
Richard Clay (The Chaucer Press) Ltd
Bungay, Suffolk*

British Library
Cataloguing in Publication Data
Blackler, F. H. M.
    Applying psychology in organizations.
    —*(New essential psychology)*
    1. Organizational behavior
    I. Title   II. Shimmin,
    Sylvia   III. Series
302.3'5   HD58.7
ISBN 0-416-33680-9

Library of Congress
Cataloging in Publication Data
Blackler, F. H. M.
    Applying psychology in organizations.

    (New essential psychology)
    Bibliography: p.
    Includes indexes.
    1. Psychology, Industrial.
    I. Shimmin, Sylvia.
II. Title.   III. Series.
HF5548.8.B54   1984   158.7
    84-10723
ISBN 0-416-33680-9

Contents

1 Scope and definition of organizational psychology   1
2 The individual and the organization   13
3 The organization and the individual   27
4 Organizational processes and structure   45
5 Thought and action in organizational psychology   68
6 Approaches to organizational change   83
7 The quality of working life   104
8 Problems and perspectives in organizational psychology   124

Suggestions for further reading   136
References and name index   139
Subject index   147

1

Scope and definition of organizational psychology

It is well known that when you do
anything, unless you understand its
theory, its circumstances, its nature, and
its relations to other things, you will not
know the laws governing it, or know how
to do it; you will not know when or where
to put it into practice or be able to do it
well. (Mao Tse-Tung, 1937)

This book is about organizations and what psychology has to offer
to our understanding of them. In terms of the history of human
thought, psychology is still a young subject and the sphere of
organizational psychology is younger still, the first texts bearing
the title not appearing until the 1960s. Although human society
has always comprised organized units such as tribal and religious
communities, villages and city states, until this century these were
generally small and local. As Thompson (1973) points out, industrial firms usually began as local or regional firms, armies were
formed from locally recruited, locally organized and locally led
units, and hospitals and schools originated as local institutions. Of
the many changes which have taken place in the last eighty years,
one of the most profound is the growth and development of

organizations on a scale and complexity which impinge on all aspects of life. Not only are most of us born in an organizational setting and are likely to die in one, but we are educated in organizations, work in them, and depend on them for a host of goods and services such as food supplies, water, heating, lighting, transport and entertainment, which we are apt to take for granted unless there is a breakdown due to technical failure, industrial unrest or political upheaval. At such times, our interdependence on national and cross-national organizations becomes immediately apparent, as does the limited ability of individuals *per se* to alter the situation. It is not surprising, therefore, that behaviour in organizations has become a field of study in its own right, reflecting an increasing awareness that understanding of the nature of organizations, and of the resulting interactions between people operating in different environments, is fundamental to policy-making of all kinds. Furthermore, within this context it is now recognized that effective social regulation depends on the reconciliation of divergent and conflicting interests.

What are organizations?

Although they are so all-pervasive, organizations are not easily defined. Indeed, it has been suggested that it is more helpful to cite specific examples than to try and define the term. Proponents of this approach would point to a familiar chain-store, manufacturing company, hospital or local authority and tell us that 'these are organizations' so that, just as children learn concepts through constant naming of examples, we should understand their meaning by demonstration. Others, such as Bell (1967), have used a similar technique, asking people to compare a social gathering like a cocktail party with a work department of an industrial enterprise in order to discover the distinguishing features of an organization. This is a good way to stimulate thought and discussion, but it does not obviate the need for a formal definition. For our purposes, a convenient one with which to start is the working definition given by Schein (1980) and reproduced from the earlier editions of his text-book on organizational psychology:

An organization is the rational co-ordination of the activities of a number of people for the achievement of some common explicit purpose or goal, through division of labour and function, and through a hierarchy of authority and responsibility. (Schein, 1980, p. 15)

This definition embodies much of the traditional view of organizations. It refers specifically to those which are formally established for a given purpose, in which the co-ordination of people's activities is consciously directed and planned. It does not refer to social units, such as families and friendship groups, which emerge spontaneously from social interaction. The focus is the larger, complex groupings deliberately set up to accomplish a specific task which, by implication, is beyond the scope of both individuals and small groups. As Thompson puts it, 'we joined in the particular configurations called complex organizations because we believed it was to our advantage to do so – that our resources could be mobilised and allocated more effectively through such organization than otherwise' (Thompson, 1973, p. 328). In other words, organizations are purposive, human creations.

The patterned activities which are co-ordinated and integrated in an organization are repeated, relatively enduring, and bounded in space and time. If one visits a school, a bank, a job centre today and again tomorrow, next week and next month, one will find the same cycle of activities occurring, although the personnel concerned may not be identical. The pattern of the cycle is likely to alter over time and an important aspect of the study of organizations is to discover how and why this occurs, but a significant feature of organizations is their constancy under conditions of changing individual membership. Therefore, an organization may be described in terms of the standardized forms of behaviour associated with each task or function, that is in terms of 'roles' which must be fulfilled in order to achieve the organizational objectives. Provided that the functional requirements of these roles are met it does not matter who fulfils them, at least in principle, although in practice it may make a lot of difference to the quality of performance. The patient seeking treatment for toothache is well aware of the difference between a brusque and considerate dentist, although the function performed by each is the same. In an organization, the extent to which the occupant of a given role can change or shape it is usually limited; one of the objects of a clear job description is to ensure that, if one person leaves and is replaced by another, the newcomer will perform the same activities as the individual previously occupying that role.

There is a large body of literature on organizations which adopts the perspective outlined above – that is, which sees organizations in terms of formal, rational, planned activities to achieve specific objectives. However, such a view is more characteristic of writers in other disciplines than psychologists. The latter have been more concerned with the needs which people seek to satisfy in and through organizations and with the 'informal organization', that is the social relations and interactions which occur over and above those required by the formally prescribed roles. The emphasis, in this context, is usually on the characteristics and behaviour of individuals and small groups in organizations, rather than on the nature and structure of organizations *per se*.

Organizations as open systems

In the last decades, increasing attention has been paid to the relationship between organizations and their environments as the result of the impact of 'systems thinking' (Emery, 1969). This maintains that human organizations are living systems and should be analysed accordingly as 'open systems', that is as open to matter-energy exchanges with an environment. The starting point of this approach, therefore, is the identification and mapping of the repeated cycles of input, transformation, output and renewed input which comprise the organizational pattern. A manufacturing firm, for example, takes in people and raw materials in order to turn out a product which it sells, and the monetary return is used to obtain more labour and materials and maintain the plant so that the whole cycle of activities can be perpetuated. Similarly, a university or college, in the words of Miller and Rice,

> imports students, teaches them and provides them with opportunities to learn; it exports ex-students who have either acquired some qualification or failed. The proportion that qualifies and the standard the individuals are perceived to have attained determine the extent to which the environment provides students and resources to maintain the enterprise. (Miller and Rice, 1967, p. 3)

In yet other organizations, such as voluntary societies – Katz and Kahn (1978) cite the example of an ornithological society – the activities provided for members can be sufficiently rewarding in themselves to re-energize and ensure their continuation. Thus, organizations differ considerably in their source of energy renewal, with most utilizing internal and external sources to a varying degree, although large-scale organizations, in particular, are very dependent on their external environment. For example, the over-capacity for steel-making throughout the world has led to difficulties for steel manufacturers in many countries. In Britain, public sector organizations such as hospitals in the National Health Service, are subject to financial pressures when central government seeks to reduce public expenditure.

One of the consequences of the open systems perspective is that it is basically concerned with problems of relationship and of interdependence, rather than with the constant properties of elements. It focuses attention on a number of complex issues, such as the boundaries of systems, where one ends and the next begins, and who and what belong to which system. Within this approach, the emphasis is on multi-causality and temporal, as well as spatial, relationships and interactions. Organizations, in this sense, may be conceived as structures of events rather than of physical objects, a useful antidote to the tendency to reify them, that is to regard them as beings with a mind and a will of their own. It does not mean, however, that organizations have no physical entity. As Ackoff (1969) observes, whether or not an entity with parts is considered as a system depends on whether or not we are concerned with the behaviour of the parts and their interactions. We may also note that, experientially, members of organizations often feel that 'the company', 'the university' or whatever, is a single entity, separate from and over against them, although cognitively they know perfectly well that they are parts of that entity.

An open systems view of organizations is not confined to psychologists and is seen by some as leading to multi-disciplinary convergence. Katz and Kahn (1978), who are strong advocates of this approach, maintain 'that social psychological principles can be applied to all forms of collective organised effort is now acknowledged in many disciplines'. Nicholson and Wall (1982) go further and argue that organizational psychologists themselves are showing an increasing eclecticism and 'healthy disregard' for disciplinary boundaries.

However, just as Katz and Kahn warn, although an organization lives by being open to its environment, this does not mean *complete* openness or the organization would cease to exist (because it would be undifferentiated from its surroundings), so it is important that what is distinctively psychological in the increasingly eclectic area of organizational behaviour is recognized and distinguishable from other disciplinary approaches. Concentration on multi-disciplinary convergence, valuable though this is, may obscure from psychology students the breadth and diversity of psychological contributions to the field. Some idea of the extent of these is given by Dunnette's (1976) *Handbook of Industrial and Organizational Psychology*, a large volume of 1740 pages dealing with 37 topics, the author noting in his preface four more areas of potential concern which he has not included!

From industrial to organizational psychology

The title of Dunnette's handbook and the adoption, in 1973, of the name 'Division of Industrial and Organizational Psychology' by Division 14 of the American Psychological Association (instead of the Division of Industrial Psychology as formerly) indicate that the subject as we know it today emerged from the sub-discipline of industrial psychology. There is a great deal of conventional wisdom, not to say folk-lore, about early industrial psychology and the influences on its development which derive largely from highly condensed historical accounts in many text-books. These inevitably distort by over-simplification and we do not propose to add to their number here. Instead, we shall illustrate the transition from 'industrial' to 'organizational' psychology as it occurred in Britain, noting the somewhat different course of developments in the USA. In both countries, however, the impact of problems and applications in the two world wars was considerable.

It was the adverse effects of the extremely long hours worked by munition workers in Britain during the First World War which led to a series of important psychological studies in industry. Lupton (1966) describes these as the first researches of any consequence into problems of large-scale industrial organizations. Attempts to meet the troops' ever-increasing demand for munitions by extending the hours worked, such that 90 hours a week was common and 100 hours not unknown, resulted in decreased output and increasing rates of absence from sickness and other causes. As a result, the Health of Munition Workers' Committee was set up in 1915, 'To consider and advise on questions of industrial fatigue, hours of labour, and other matters affecting the personal health and efficiency of workers in munition factories and workshops'.

The committee's reports are difficult to obtain and are not described in detail in most of the standard texts, although its work is widely recognized as a landmark contribution in the development of industrial psychology. This was continued after the war by the Industrial Fatigue (later Health) Research Board and, at about the same time, an independent, non-profit making organization, the National Institute of Industrial Psychology (NIIP), was established by C.S. Myers, perhaps the most eminent of the founding fathers of British psychology, to promote 'the study of the human side of labour' and to put the results of such studies into practice.

Some idea of how these early investigators viewed their work, their background and experiences can be gained from the series of autobiographical articles published in *Occupational Psychology*, a journal published by the NIIP, during 1948–50. These show clearly the sense of pioneering which suffused their contributors' work and the challenge presented by industrial psychology. For example, H.M. Vernon (1948), who demonstrated by the output data he collected the advantages of reducing the long hours in the munition factories, reveals that he himself spent two months as a munition worker earlier in the war and that 'it altered the whole course of my life'. He notes, in particular, the lack of consideration shown by management to the workers. When invited to be the first investigator for the Industrial Fatigue Research Board he reports 'I had no hesitation in accepting the invitation. I never regretted my decision for I considered that industry offered an immense but largely neglected field for useful research', even though it meant relinquishing his Oxford academic appointments, which his friends thought very foolish. Dr Vernon also records his disappointment that, in the earlier stages of the Second World War, some of the chief lessons learnt during the First World War about hours of work were almost ignored.

The same point is made by Wyatt (1950) who, in outlining the course of 'a long and interesting series of adventures in the unexplored field of industrial psychology', comments that

Our work during the war was, on the whole, scrappy and disappointing. After the fall of Dunkirk the emphasis was on output regardless of the wear and tear on workers and machines. Almost all the findings of the previous twenty years were completely ignored and for a time the hours of work in many factories were from 70 to 80 per week. Workers throughout the country were urged and inspired to make good the material losses incurred as a result of the collapse of France and there was an immediate and substantial rise in weekly output. The vigorous spirit at the beginning of the long race for output soon began to wane and it did more harm than good. . . . It was a valiant but misguided effort and the effects were noticeable long after the hours of work had been reduced. (Wyatt, 1950, p. 72)

This illustrates a fundamental problem in applying psychology in organizations, namely the extent to which psychological knowledge is acceptable as a basis for action by policy makers and managers when it runs counter to 'common-sense', 'natural' assumptions or short-term expediency. It also shows the impact of environmental factors on behaviour in organizations and the reciprocal effects of external and internal influences.

Other contributions by British psychologists in the First World War included the development and application of psychological tests for specific tasks such as those devised by C.S. Myers in selecting men to use the hydrophone to detect enemy submarines. But it was in the USA that psychological testing for vocational purposes took place on a mass scale. As Dunnette and Borman (1979) record, the modern era of personnel selection dates from 1917 when the USA declared war on Germany. American Psychological Association psychologists were urged to give professional assistance to the war effort and, shortly afterwards, two groups of army psychologists were formed. Within less than two years well over one million men were tested. In addition, job specifications were written, job knowledge (trade tests) invented, officer-rating forms devised and counselling programmes mounted.

These two traditions in industrial psychology, of investigations into hours and conditions of work, on the one hand, and of selection and vocational guidance, on the other, were maintained in Britain in the inter-war period under the auspices of the Industrial Health Research Board and the National Institute of Industrial Psychology respectively. Both extended their areas of study later to include attitude surveys. The same period also saw fundamental work in the universities relating to applied problems, notably at Cambridge on man-machine relationships. A common thread in all these developments was a concern with efficiency, associated with the belief that commercial success and occupational health rested on deploying human resources most effectively, a formulation often expressed in Britain as 'fitting the man to the job – fitting the job to the man' (fmj-fjm).

Meanwhile, the well-known 'Hawthorne studies' were carried out at the Hawthorne works of the General Electric Company in Chicago in the late 1920s and early 1930s. Beginning as investigations of the effects of different intensities of illumination on output (i.e. classic industrial psychology experiments), these had unexpected results which focused attention on workers' responses to the studies themselves and to the nature of industrial work groups. Their influence on subsequent industrial social psychology, and on managerial thought and practice represented by the 'human relations' movement has been tremendous and we shall return to these topics later. Here, we simply wish to note that the Hawthorne investigations are probably the most widely cited and least read in their entirety of all studies in this field. Partial accounts abound and, latterly, some severe criticisms have been made of this work which, to be properly understood, need to be compared with what the original investigators did and said (Roethlisberger and Dickson, 1939).

These studies are of major importance because, whatever their limitations, they led to a changed view of people at work. It is difficult to realize now how revolutionary were the findings that workers have their own perceptions and interpretations of events, norms of conduct and performance and ways of sanctioning their co-workers – that they are sentient beings and not mere 'cogs in a machine'. That this now seems self-evident is a measure of the change in outlook since the 1920s, a change which has not necessarily entailed concomitant changes in work structures.

The contributions of British psychologists to the problems of selection, training and design of jobs in the Second World War, and to the associated problems of, first, adjustment to service life and, later, civil re-settlement, foreshadowed a number of post-war developments. As a result of the group procedures for officer selection used by the War Office Selection Boards, a situational approach to leadership was adopted by large companies after the war in selecting management trainees. The Civil Service

Selection Board likewise operated on these lines. Analysis of complex skills and the design of equipment and information displays in aircraft cockpits to minimize pilot error laid the foundations of ergonomics and the application of this approach to industrial problems. A direct consequence of the war, as Eunice Belbin (1979) pointed out in her 1978 Myers lecture to the British Psychological Society, was that psychology students in the immediate post-war years were taught by academics with a great fund of experience in the application of psychology. To her and her contemporaries at Cambridge at the time, 'That psychology was applicable to the wide range of problems that surrounded us in the outside world, was something we never had occasion to doubt'. Twenty years later this view was to be found in business schools rather than in university departments of psychology. Tizard's theme in his presidential address to the British Psychological Society in 1976 was the failure, as he saw it, of academic psychologists to address themselves to the problems of everyday life.

An important development for organizational psychology was the establishment after the war of the Tavistock Institute of Human Relations as a sister institute to the Tavistock Clinic (a voluntary out-patient clinic for psychotherapy founded in 1920). Much of the wartime work on selection, service training, the civil re-settlement of repatriated prisoners-of-war and the development of therapeutic communities for those who had suffered breakdown had involved staff from the Tavistock Clinic, who constituted a multi-disciplinary group of psychiatrists, psychologists, sociologists and anthropologists. This group felt that the combined approach to practical problems developed during the war was equally applicable to peacetime issues and that they were responsible for some major innovations in organizational research.

Key elements of the Institute's research approach were that it was problem-centred and entailed a professional responsibility to the 'client' organization. Action research, as it is usually called, is based on quite a different model of research from that of conventional applied research. Instead of the expert who works with scientific detachment and reports the results for action by others, the researcher and client engage in a joint commitment and share responsibility for the outcome and application of the research findings. It is an approach which transcends disciplinary boundaries, but which also places psychologists and social scientists in situations of role ambiguity, power struggles, negotiation, differing values and expectations. Such problems of professional practice are not well documented and are relatively little discussed. For a graphic account of the experiences of a social scientist in British industry see Klein (1976) and, for a transatlantic perspective, the report of the American Psychological Association's Task Force on the Practice of Psychology in Industry (1971).

Many industrial psychologists in the post-war years continued to assume a 'technical service' role, seeking to employ the methods of their discipline to find a technical solution to problems presented to them by their clients or employer. In the 1960s, as new organizational problems associated with growth and changing employee expectations came to the fore, they began to feel that an over-concentration on traditional concerns (e.g. selection and training) and an exclusive reliance on traditional methodologies (based on experimentation or on social survey techniques) were somewhat limiting. There was increased awareness of the need to extend their focus, not only from the individual to the small group but also to the organization and the wider environment and, in so doing, to take account of the concepts and approaches of other disciplines.

Even so, the search for a more meaningful and more socially relevant orientation to meet the challenges of the latter part of the century has been a difficult process. Confronted with problems outside their traditional areas of expertise for which there are no straightforward technical solutions, such as structural unemployment, pollution, the training needs of developing countries, to name but a few, industrial and organizational psychologists have been uncertain as to which direction to take. Some have retreated into academic ivory towers, less secure now than formerly, while others have become immersed in multi-disciplinary, organizational studies. It has been suggested that what is needed to prepare us for the future is learning to cope with transience, that is with the accelerating changes that are occurring throughout society as a result of social, political, economic and technological upheavals and developments. For individuals, groups and organizations these mean that instability and impermanence are characteristic features of their environments with which they must cope and to which they must adapt successfully. This is recognizable as a psychological problem, albeit an extremely challenging one, and it is in this context that the following chapters should be read.

In a short text, it is difficult to cover what is now an enormous subject, as Dunnette's (1976) massive handbook indicates. We focus, therefore, on some key issues that have attracted particular attention from psychologists and seek to show, with examples from British research, how organizational psychology has developed and is continuing to develop. Chapters 2 and 3 deal with the relation between individuals and organizations, first in terms of what individuals expect from organizations, especially those which employ them, and then from the perspective of the ways in which organizations seek to attract, engage and utilize people in achieving organizational objectives. These chapters and chapter 4, which is concerned with the social processes that occur in organizations and related issues of structure, are rooted in the more traditional, psychological approaches to the study of individuals and groups, but draw also on sociological contributions, where appropriate.

In chapter 5 we turn, more specifically, to organizational psychology in theory and practice showing how, like other areas of applied psychology, it is not immune from a divergence of outlook between scientists and practitioners. Chapters 6 and 7 are concerned with applications made in the last twenty years which have not only increased our understanding of behaviour in organizations but also led to the maturing and greater sophistication of organizational psychology as a discipline. Finally, in chapter 8, we review current developments and identify a number of issues of social concern to which psychology can be expected to make a significant contribution in the future.

2

The individual
and the organization

No matter what you have to do with an
organization – whether you are going to
study it, work in it, consult for it, subvert it
or use it in the interest of another
organization – you must have some view of
the nature of the beast with which you are
dealing. (Perrow, 1970, p. 1)

Individual perspectives

The above statement applies to everyone, whether or not a
person's involvement with an organization is active, as the quotation suggests, or passive in the sense that it occurs at the discretion
of others and/or because it is a legal requirement as, for example,
with army conscripts. Most of the literature on organizational
membership assumes that it is a matter of choice. This means that
far more research has been done on people's expectations of, and
responses to, the organizations they join as adults, particularly
those in which they seek or obtain employment, than on antece-
dent learning about organizations in childhood and adolescence.
But it is as institutions which provide goods and services (schools,
hospitals, shops, bus companies, etc.) and control behaviour

(licensing authorities, rent and tax collection, law enforcement, etc.) that people first encounter organizations. For the majority, this occurs initially through compulsory education, which combines both elements, placing children in the position of recipients of what others have decreed they should be taught and in what ways. Early experience of organizations is of corporate bodies, external to and separate from individuals, with which the latter must engage in particular ways for particular purposes. Voluntary commitment, that is 'joining' an organization, may occur first in youth clubs and interest groups, the formal transition to organizational membership as an active contributor to the provision of goods and services being associated, traditionally, with leaving school and entry into employment.

Because they are ubiquitous in developed societies, organizations have an important influence on people's lives in a number of ways. *First*, they are the context in which we develop concepts of ourselves and the world about us. Social learning occurs largely within organizations as it is in these settings that we experience competition, collaboration, the exercise of power and authority and the various ways in which individuals and groups seek to influence and control one another. *Second*, but related to the above, the temporal sequence of our lives and our social status relate to the organizations we expect to move through over time, for example school, place of work, leisure centre, hockey club and perhaps, ultimately, old people's home. How we define ourselves and how others perceive us are indicated by such general titles as pupil, student, senior citizen and so on, as well as by the more specific occupational titles such as fitter, doctor, teacher, to which may be attached the name of the employing organization, for example, fitter with North West Gas. Therefore a *third* aspect of organizations is that, from an individual viewpoint, they are providers – of education, employment, career opportunities, therapy, residential care – that is they are the means through which a person hopes to achieve particular ends and, as such, may meet or frustrate his or her needs and aspirations.

In this chapter we shall concentrate on the individual's experience of work organizations as it is these to which psychologists and other social scientists have given most attention. It should be noted, however, that the characteristics of entry and assimilation into membership and their consequences apply equally to non-work organizations.

Entering organizations

Newcomers to organizations face unfamiliar situations which present them with experiences of change, contrast, surprise and the need to make sense of their new surroundings. They have to 'learn the ropes', that is to assimilate the culture, during the period of socialization which marks their transition from outsider to insider. This process of assimilation is complete when, in their own eyes and those of their peers, they are no longer distinct from established members and are freely admitted to the gossip and informal networks. As Burns and Stalker (1966) put it, 'until it is other places which begin to have a disconcertingly unfamiliar smell' newcomers 'have neither been accepted nor accepted their position'. In some instances, the process is marked by rituals, such as formal welcomes and introductions, induction training programmes and the like, or informal teasing, joking and even mild forms of horseplay to which new apprentices and others may be subjected. These 'initiation rites', as anthropologists refer to them, serve to indicate that the 'belongingness' experienced as a member of an organization is not to be taken for granted, but is only acquired when the individual is accepted by his or her immediate associates. 'Intensification rites', such as office parties, act as reinforcers of full membership, as do the 'rites of passage' or farewell ceremonies held for those who leave.

How people respond to these practices, and to the continuous socializing influences to which they are exposed by virtue of their organizational membership, depends largely on why they joined the organization concerned and the value they attach to it. For example, there is a vast difference between the behaviour of trade union members who belong to the union solely because of a closed shop agreement, but never attend a union meeting, and that of political activists for whom the union is a major interest and to which they devote most of their time and energy. People differ considerably in how much of themselves they are prepared to give to an organization, not least because institutions differ in the demands their constituent roles make upon individuals. In the world of work there is a range from those whose 'central life interests' lie outside their place of work, and whose commitment to their jobs is minimal, to the 'organization men' for whom their work occupies almost all their 'life-space'. Even in coercive institutions, where people cannot withdraw physically from the situation, their thoughts and fantasies extend far beyond it. For this reason, the term 'partial inclusion' has been used to denote the fact that, while individuals may be physically present and carrying out their required duties, their thoughts and feelings may lie elsewhere and what really concerns and motivates them may be outside the organization's control.

The initial period of employment, during which people are trying to 'find their feet' in the organization, is sometimes referred to as the 'induction crisis'. Studies of labour turnover show that it is often high during this period when people have not developed sufficiently strong links with the organization to cause them to remain if other opportunities are available. Although the propensity to stay or leave is affected by the state of the job market, family circumstances and other factors, survival of the 'induction crisis' for many people means the beginning of an attachment to the organization so that the longer they work for it the less likely they are to leave voluntarily.

As we shall see in the next chapter, organizations are concerned that their members should be committed, not least because turnover and the recruitment and training of replacements for those who leave can be very costly. A great deal of psychological research has been directed towards discovering how and why people become attached to both their jobs and their organizations, with a view to strengthening employee-organization linkages. It should be noted, however, that there are two sides to this issue. Whereas psychologists employed to help reduce labour turnover in an organization are likely to view it in managerial terms as a form of 'wastage', if they are employed as counsellors to individuals who are unhappy in their work, they may perceive that leaving the organization and seeking alternative employment or training would be in a person's best interests.

The psychological contract

People therefore enter organizations for different reasons and with different orientations as a result of their previous experience and present circumstances. In work organizations they undertake specific tasks for an agreed payment, that is they put their time and talents at the disposal of their employer for a fixed period at a price determined by negotiation. This is recognized in the formal contract of employment, but a 'psychological contract' is also involved. This is essentially a set of expectations about the nature of the exchange between the individual and the organization. When a person takes up a job, he or she has a variety of expectations of the organization and the organization has a variety of expectations of the person. Many of these expectations are implicit and unstated, but they act as powerful determinants of behaviour. Included in the psychological contract are the subtleties of how people expect to be treated, in mode of address, consideration and recognition, for example, where manner or tone of voice may be interpreted by one or other of the parties as falling short of their expectations. Thus an individual may feel ignored, exploited or a 'mere cog in a machine' while the organization, as represented by a manager or foreman, may regard the employee as lazy, uncooperative or rude. The motivation to work is closely bound up with the establishment of an effective psychological contract, that is an agreement between the individual and the organization, through a process of mutual bargaining, as to what is to be given and received, together with subsequent honouring of this agreement.

The concept of a psychological contract applies also to non-work organizations. Levinson (1972), for example, gives the illustration of a church in which the members have become inward-looking, fiercely attached to the church and to each other and who therefore feel that their contract is being violated when their pastor puts pressure on them to become involved in outside affairs and wider denominational institutions. It is also relevant to the activities of consumer groups and similar bodies which seek to articulate and achieve a better match between the needs and expectations of customers, patients, users and clients and the provisions made for them by the various service organizations. The present imbalance between the ideas of the providers and those of the receivers is reflected in the following observation from the Good Food Guide section of the *Guardian* (15 October 1982). Referring to the failure of some restaurants to 'match the state of the art, as a chef sees it, to the desires of a customer, as the customer sees it', the article continues: 'It is of course always wise to remember, as you cross the threshold, that of all institutions a restaurant most closely resembles a hospital: in other words, it is organized not for the customers' convenience but for its own.' This raises the question of on whose behalf such organizations operate and how one can or should negotiate the double psychological contract involved, that is between the organization, as an employer, and its staff, and the organization, as a provider, and the recipients of its care or services. For example, lining-up or queueing for a bus, for service at a post-office counter or bank, or for attention in an outpatients' department, may be an arrangement which both employers and employees see as facilitating a workable psychological contract between them and their passengers, customers and patients, but which the latter regard as falling short of their expectations of good or even satisfactory services.

From the individual's viewpoint, the implicit contract made with organizations is not a contract of equals. The balance of power lies with the organization and, in employment relationships, people are expected, and they themselves expect, to conform to administrative rules, task structures and norms of behaviour. These may reflect wider social norms and prevailing stereotypes about the division of labour and the capabilities of disadvantaged groups. For example, many women expect to be given few, if any, opportunities for further training and advancement in comparison with their male colleagues, so discriminatory action of this kind by their employers is perceived as inevitable. In other words, the psychological contracts of people of low social status are likely to rest on low expectations of the treatment they will receive, which may be matched by low evaluations of their potential by the organizations concerned. This was one of the features that made a deep impression on a Swedish author and poet who spent a year working in a factory. Palm (1977) notes that the majority of unskilled or semi-skilled factory workers, whose occupations put them at the bottom of the labour market, often 'lower the level of their demands, limit their territory, keep out of the way when things begin to get hot, satisfy themselves with accepting what is offered, reduce their ambitions and transfer their remaining hopes from their work to their leisure time'. He comments:

> We talk about administrators 'making a career', about graduates and artists as being 'talented' or as being 'successful', about craftsmen and specialised workers as being 'skilled', etc. But who ever heard of an assembly line worker who 'made a career' I mean just precisely as an assembly line worker? Of a (fork-lift) truck driver who 'is successful' in his occupation? Of a store assistant who 'gets on' without leaving his or her store? (Palm 1977, p. 83)

In his opinion, the low evaluation accorded to these occupations by society as a whole inevitably colours the expectations of both parties to the psychological contract for such work. Palm writes on the basis of his personal experience and as a poet, not as a social scientist. But his observations are both challenging and pertinent to psychological perspectives on entry into employment, organizational commitment and career development, many of which rest on concepts of skilled or professional work.

Occupational choice and career development

Entry into employment is often referred to as occupational choice, although the extent to which individuals are able to consider alternatives and decide between different options varies greatly. Vroom (1964) distinguishes between *occupational preferences* (the occupations which are most attractive to individuals), *occupational choices* (those toward which they are most strongly impelled) and *occupational attainments* (the occupations actually entered), which together constitute the 'occupational choice process'. This formulation recognizes that the jobs people enter may not be those which attract them and that, in times of high unemployment, occupational attainment may be zero, regardless of preference or choice. It also accords with the views of other writers that the occupational choice process extends over a long period, culminating in an outcome which represents complex interactions between personal, social and economic factors.

Although a number of theories of vocational choice centre on the concept of the choosing person, Super and Bohn (1971) point out that such an individual is essentially middle-class. For the socially disadvantaged and members of minority groups jobs are not chosen in any positive sense, because people have to take what is open to them. Indeed, Roberts (1977) thinks this applies to the majority of the labour force. However, one can see evidence of negative choice in developed societies where social welfare provision is such that people do not feel that 'any job is better than no job'. Certain jobs are then rejected by many of the nationals and are filled by 'guest workers' from developing countries, as in European assembly plants, or by immigrants, as in British manufacturing industry. This rejection indicates that, whatever their circumstances, people have some notions of what jobs they would prefer and those they do not wish to undertake. In expressing such preferences, Super and Bohn (1971) argue, individuals are stating, in occupational terms, the kinds of people they hope to be; the whole process of entering employment, becoming established in or changing jobs, is to be understood in terms of the formation, translation and implementation of individuals' self-concepts. From this perspective, career development is a life-time process of 'self-implementation' in which the self-concept, formed early in life, is tested against reality and modified through occupational choice, employment experience and beyond it: careers 'begin before employment, are shaped by parental (and social background) educational opportunities, etc. . . . and extend into retirement' (Super and Bohn, 1971, p. 117). The main stages of this process are shown in table 1.

Schein (1980) reports support for a developmental approach of this kind from a longitudinal study he made of male graduates from a leading American management school. He found that many of these men did not achieve a clear self-image until they had been in an occupational environment for several years, covering different jobs and organizations, through which they discovered and sought to reconcile matches and mismatches between their own needs, values and talents and the requirements of their employing organizations. The search for a clear and workable self-concept, Schein suggests, may well continue throughout life and, therefore, to look for a single set of motives or values that determine choice of occupation or entry into a specific type of employment is to take a restricted view of the subjective

Table 1   Career development as implementation of the self-concept

---

(1) Exploration: childhood and adolescent development of the self-concept;
(2) Reality testing: transition from school to work or work-experience programmes;
(3) Trial and experimentation: attempts to implement the self-concept by staking out adult roles and career(s);
(4) Establishment: stabilizing and modifying the self-concept through the early and mid-career years;
(5) Maintenance: preserving and continuing to implement the self-concept in accordance with established pattern;
(6) Decline: adjustments to self-concept as result of ageing and retirement.

After Schein's (1980) account of Super and Bohn's (1971) theory.

aspects of the experience and their significance for the individual. Although a tentative self-concept develops in childhood and adolescence, largely through interactions with 'significant others', it is not until adulthood that this can be tested, modified and stabilized, largely through work and work-related activities.

Law (1981) provides a useful overview of the ways in which theories of and approaches to career-development have changed over the years in response to changing social conditions, with particular reference to contemporary Britain. He contrasts the developmental approaches of psychologists, focused on internally experienced needs, aspirations and feelings, with the situational approaches of sociologists, focused on external factors of rewards and opportunities in a socially stratified society, and argues that neither perspective is adequate on its own: 'The events of motivated career development cannot be described wholly in the psychological terms of needs pursued, nor wholly in the sociological terms of incentives offered. Instead, a great deal of the process of identifying motivation for career development occurs in mid-range transactions involving the participation of parents, family, neighbourhood, peer groups and ethnic group' (Law, 1981, p. 149), that is through exchanges between individuals and the groups of which they are members. Law uses the term 'community interaction' for this 'mid-range' focus for theories of career development, which he sees as bridging the gap between 'self' and 'situation' approaches and facilitating understanding of the 'senses in which neither self nor situation are fixed and absolute in their influence upon what people do'. His ideas, illustrated in figure 1, provide a framework which encompasses experiences outside and preceding employment, as well as those within the work organization and the meanings these have for the individual.

Self and role

The positions occupied in the course of a career are often described in terms of the roles which people are required to play in filling these positions, that is the specified patterns of behaviour associated with the jobs in question. People may find their roles comfortable and congenial or a source of stress and conflict. Thus, they may feel that their behaviour and image of themselves

21

Figure 1 Influences upon career development. (After Law, 1981)

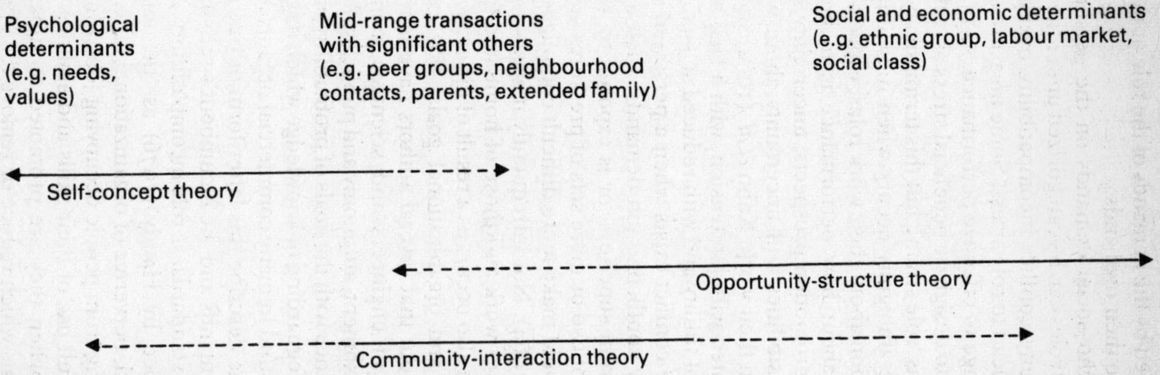

Psychological determinants
(e.g. needs, values)

Self-concept theory

Mid-range transactions with significant others
(e.g. peer groups, neighbourhood contacts, parents, extended family)

Community-interaction theory

Social and economic determinants
(e.g. ethnic group, labour market, social class)

Opportunity-structure theory

is shaped by the demands of the role or they may seek to shape the latter to their own ends.

Psycho-social demands on the person arising from organizational roles can be categorized under the following headings: role ambiguity, conflict, incompatibility, overload and underload, all of which lead to role stress. Some measure of stress may provide the challenge to effective performance, so that Handy (1976) finds it useful to designate beneficial stress as 'role pressure' and harmful stress as 'role strain', but this terminology is by no means general.

Role ambiguity occurs when individuals have inadequate information about their work roles, especially in the form of uncertainty about how performance is to be evaluated, uncertainty about promotion prospects, uncertainty about the extent of their responsibilities and uncertainty about what others expect from them in their work. Kahn *et al.* (1964) showed that ambiguity was associated with job tension, with a lack of job satisfaction, with a sense of futility and with reduced self-confidence.

Role conflict exists when a person in a particular work role is torn by conflicting job demands, such as contradictory instructions from superiors, or is exposed to 'the simultaneous occurrence of two or more sets of pressures such that compliance with one would make more difficult compliance with the other' (Kahn *et al.*, 1964). Not infrequently it arises from a clash between the claims of work and those of home and family on an individual's time. It also occurs as a result of differences between professional values and organizational goals. For example, Keenan (1980) points out that several authors have noted how the professional values of engineers and scientists, emphasizing technical accomplishment, autonomy and public availability of knowledge, are at variance with the goals of profitability, marketability of products and safeguarding of knowledge which might be useful to competitors, found in many commercial organizations.

Some describe this latter form of role conflict, that is between role demands and the incumbent's self-image, personal values or ethical standards, as role incompatibility. A particular form of this, described by Handy (1976) as 'the most insidious, but most ignored, perverter of organizational efficiency', is role underload resulting from people occupying jobs which do not allow them to make full use of their skills and abilities. Paradoxically, this may occur when they are promoted to supervisory or management positions which reduce or remove the opportunity to do the work for which they were trained and with which they identify. Professionals and skilled craft workers are particularly prone to this type of conflict, for example nurses whose contact with patients lessens with increasing seniority and engineers for whom advancement means abandoning technical work for management.

Excessive demands or role overload may be both quantitative, in the sense of having too much to do in the time available, or qualitative in the sense of having to act on inadequate information or accomplish a task for which the person feels ill-prepared and/or without the requisite materials. Here again, this may be experienced largely as a result of the individual's own attitudes. The perfectionist, for example, whose self-esteem is tied closely to the idea of a job well done, is likely to be more subject to stress of this kind than someone who is happy-go-lucky in his or her approach. As Keenan (1980) says of professional engineers, 'the successful accomplishment of meaningful technical work is at the centre of their perception of themselves in their jobs'. Consequently, neither work that under-utilizes their technical skills nor work that is so demanding that they feel unable to complete it successfully is satisfactory from their point of view.

One of the problems of role-related conflicts and stresses of these kinds is that many of the organizational effects on individuals are not easily observed and are confounded by the effects of other roles and experiences. People enact many roles, such as manager, husband, father, chess-player, amateur footballer, each of which imposes its stresses and offers its rewards, to which they respond in different ways. There is also the tendency in affluent societies for the role of consumer to acquire increasing prominence. For those to whom 'conspicuous consumption' becomes a measure of success and social esteem, work roles may be evaluated in terms of monetary return rather than their intrinsic content or opportunities for personal development.

Work and organizations

Implicit in the foregoing sections is the idea of a work society, that is one built around jobs, so that our concepts of ourselves and our social positions are defined in terms of our work roles. In this context, work is equated with paid employment and especially with formal paid employment in large, bureaucratic organizations. It is primarily through their jobs that individuals contribute towards the provision of goods and services for others to enjoy. What they achieve in their work helps them to develop self-respect and a feeling of personal worth. Moreover, it is principally through their work that people acquire their social status and standing in a community. Thus, when people explain to newly made acquaintances who they are, it is most unlikely that they will say 'I'm an amateur pianist' or 'an Agatha Christie reader' or 'a DIY enthusiast'. Usually they will refer to their work in describing who they are: 'a plumber', 'a housewife', 'a secretary', 'a teacher'. Or else they will refer to their employing organization: 'I work at X's'. For, as Wilensky (1960) pointed out over twenty years ago, automation and increasing refinements in the division of labour have made many jobs 'status-invisible' because they carry no name by which a person may be recognized. These workers, therefore, get their status and identification not from the work they do, but from the organizations for which they work. One of the deprivations of the unemployed is the absence of these sources of identity, especially if no occupational title can be claimed and people are unable to describe themselves as, say, 'an unemployed electrician' or 'a former teacher'.

Most authorities are now agreed, however, that previous assumptions about a 'job for life' and the possibility of an uninterrupted, ordered career within a given occupation are no longer tenable. Although, at any one time, the majority of the population will probably be in employment, an increasing number of us can expect short or long periods of unemployment in our life-time. Those who have studied the problem and its psychological implications feel that, in the interests of individuals and society, this calls for a change in our concepts of work whereby it is no longer defined in terms of employment but includes all purposive and productive effort. And this means, according to Hearn (1981), challenging two central values of careers guidance, namely the central importance of work as employment and the central value of working for an organization. He suggests that the changing social values of the 1960s, the rise of social politics and feminism, the growth of trade-union power, and the development of protest within the public sector, welfare and middle-class occupations, have all undermined the value which people attach to particular organizations and organizations in general. Therefore, alternative definitions of work such as self-help projects, community activities and the like, need establishing as sources of identity and social status through which individuals may be encouraged to explore their images of themselves and their aspirations.

The same point is made by a number of writers on the self-concept and self-theory. Bennis and Slater (1968), among others, point to the advantages of, and trend towards, self-definitions that are not rooted in social structures, while Klapp (1969) suggests that we may each need to develop a permanent 'double identity', that is one in which the self as defined by non-work activities and interests is at least as important as that defined by work, education and background. In his view, to promote psychological well-being in an 'affluent society', welfare should be aimed 'not at jobs but at purposes', so that life is meaningful independently of role and organizational commitment. At present, although the 'central life interests' of some lie outside their place of work, others identify closely with the organization's goals and values, while yet others see themselves primarily as a member of an occupational group rather than as an employee of a particular organization. For example, an accountant's self-concept may be rooted in membership of his or her profession and not in the firm for which he or she works.

However, commitment is not limited to work organizations, as football club supporters testify, but this does not mean that the effects of work organizations on their members should be neglected. In an influential book published in 1957, Argyris argued that formal organizational structures and procedures tend to inhibit personal growth and development because they encourage employees to be passive, dependent and subordinate. Since that time, as we show in chapter 7, considerable progress has been made in our understanding of how to improve the quality of working life so as to counteract these adverse tendencies. But, as Palm (1977) and others have noted, a great deal still remains to be done. We would endorse Schein's (1980) view that human motivation and career development are highly complex and not yet fully understood, so that 'a continued spirit of inquiry and a commitment to diagnosing situations before leaping into action appears to be the only safe course'. There is no ideal psychological contract that will suit all individuals or all circumstances. 'And one must be aware that personal assumptions and biases can operate as personal filters to make the world look simpler than it actually is' (Schein, 1980, p. 101).

3

The organization and the individual

What is considered occupational choice
from the standpoint of the individual
becomes the process of recruitment from
the standpoint of the profession and the
allocation of personnel in various
occupations from the standpoint of
society. What the individual defines as a
'promising opportunity' afforded by the
labour market, the profession defines as
an 'acute shortage' and the society as an
'imbalance' of occupational distribution.
(Merton *et al.*, 1957, p. 68)

Human resources

The above quotation illustrates clearly the other side of the
psychological contract which we considered from the individual's
viewpoint in the last chapter. To the organization or, more
specifically, to those members who are responsible for formulat-
ing and implementing personnel policies, people are resources
whose time and talents are to be used in achieving organizational
goals. This is illustrated by the term 'human assets accounting'
used in some management circles to signify that people may be

regarded as assets to be utilized, maintained and controlled in the same way as material assets. Thus, in recruiting and managing its human resources, an organization seeks specific abilities and attributes that can be aligned to specific job requirements; it is not concerned with, nor does it need, to develop every one of its members' potential to the full. There may even be a clash of interests, as a foundry manager observed to one of the authors when he discovered that his best apprentice was also a champion amateur racing cyclist who wanted time off for competitions.

Given the diversity of individual aims and expectations, abilities and motivation, the task of recruiting, selecting, training, controlling and maintaining people's commitment to their roles and tasks in an organization is a difficult and complex problem. Organizations, in designing and specifying jobs and seeking people to fill them, normally operate on the assumption that people are interchangeable in the sense that they are expected to fit the roles to which they are assigned. Personnel selection rests on the belief that, by careful analysis of jobs and the demands they make on individuals, it is possible to specify personnel requirements so that only those who meet the specifications for the particular job are likely to apply for it. The aim is to minimize individual differences relative to the job, hoping thereby to enhance the chances of selecting the 'right' person to fill it, that is one who will undertake the necessary tasks and duties effectively and be acceptable to co-workers and other members of the organization. People are costly resources – the more often new employees have to be recruited and trained, the more expensive it becomes, quite apart from costs arising from unsatisfactory personnel who perform their work carelessly or whose attendance is intermittent and unpredictable. It is not surprising, therefore, that there is a long tradition of psychological research directed towards facilitating good personnel decisions and effective training procedures. In this chapter we discuss work in this tradition before commenting on other influence and control strategies commonly adopted within organizations.

Recruitment and selection

The process of attracting and choosing employees occurs within the context of prevailing patterns of employment, the characteristics of the labour market and the organization's staffing policy, that is its assessment of its present resources, personnel demands over a number of years, future wastage and labour requirements and the availability of new recruits. In periods of full employment, it may be impossible to select from a number of suitable applicants, organizations being glad to take on anyone who appears eligible and willing to work for them. The emphasis is then put on training and development of the personnel available, rather than on selection procedures. Economic recession and high levels of unemployment, on the other hand, lead to an increased interest in personnel selection techniques because of the large numbers of applicants likely to put in for any vacancy.

Most of the research in this area has concentrated upon the validity of the different procedures used by organizations in making their selection decisions, that is how well interviews, psychological tests and other measures predict successful job performance. The problems of selection validation are two-fold. First, there is the fact that one never knows how well rejected candidates might have done if they had been selected, possibly better than those chosen for the job. Second, there is the criterion problem, that is how to measure the occupational success against which to judge selection predictions. The difficulty in obtaining performance measures is such that reliance is placed, in many cases, on subjective ratings by superiors, which may be far from reliable. Furthermore, as Brotherton (1980) points out, except where occupational psychologists are involved in the construction, maintenance and evaluation of selection procedures, which in Britain is usually confined to government departments, the technicalities and problems inherent in validation are often not understood.

Porter *et al.* (1975) summarize the results of research on selection as showing that unless validity coefficients are high, which is seldom, the selection ratio is high, that is the number of applicants far exceed the number of openings, and unless the jobs are difficult, which usually means higher-level jobs, selection programmes tend to produce only small increases in organizational effectiveness. They also suggest that, because both individuals and organizations are eager to impress each other in what is seen typically as a competitive situation, selection decisions often rest on misperceptions and inadequate information. In their view, the ideal situation would be one in which the organization described the advantages and disadvantages of the job on offer and perhaps allowed applicants to talk to those already doing it. The organization would feed back to candidates the results of any tests administered, indicating their significance to the job in question, while applicants, in their turn, would be more open about their strengths and weaknesses so that the prospective employer and employee could jointly assess the latter's suitability for the post.

A counselling, problem-solving approach of this kind is, as Porter and his colleagues admit, unlikely to be achieved quickly or easily, not least because it challenges traditional, unilateral decision-making by organizations in selecting their employees. However, they consider that social and legal pressures in the USA to eliminate selection procedures which discriminate between those of different races or sex may well force organizations to revise their methods of selection. Holdsworth (1983), while commenting that this is an issue which has received less attention in Britain, nevertheless identifies it as a recent trend affecting practices in this country. Another is what he calls the democratization of the selection process, that is giving greater consideration to the candidate's viewpoint and making more flexible and interactive use of different selection techniques.

As jobs have become more complex and subject to change under the impact of changing technology and as legislation prevents employers from hiring and firing at will, it becomes increasingly important for the organization to select people who will respond suitably to training or re-training rather than to concentrate on applicants' existing skills. Traditional selection methods, based on interviews and psychometric tests designed to measure abilities which may be only marginally relevant to a specific job, are not only poor predictors of the new skills required but also run the risk of discriminating against educationally and socially disadvantaged groups. A number of authors have suggested that the relatively low achievement of some members of minority groups on conventional tests is not necessarily an indicator of low potential as, given appropriate training and experience, their performance potential may be considerably higher.

One of the most promising approaches to selection developed in recent years, which offers a means of selecting people for a variety of jobs that is both technically and legally defensible, is trainability testing (Robertson and Downs, 1979). This is a specialized form of work-sample testing in which applicants are given a structured and controlled period of training in the skills they will be required to learn and are then systematically observed and rated as they attempt to carry out the task they have just been taught. Attention is paid not only to what they do but how they do it. A trainability test, therefore, is job-specific and assumes no prior knowledge or experience on the part of the applicant. Its content must be closely related to and preferably form an actual part of the job. It must also be administered in the surroundings in which successful applicants will train and work. In this way applicants learn about the work environment as well as the job itself; an additional advantage of this form of testing is that applicants are able to judge for themselves their suitability for the type of work in question. Therefore, as Downs (1980) observes, trainability tests may be regarded as condensed probationary periods.

Research conducted in Britain has shown that trainability tests can usefully be applied to a number of semi-skilled manual tasks such as sewing machining, electric arc welding, fork-lift truck operating, and so on. The concept of trainability has also been extended and used to identify potential in other areas such as manual dexterity in dentistry and management potential. This approach has the disadvantage that, for each new task, a trainability test has to be designed and validated afresh. Such tests tend to take longer to administer than paper and pencil tests. Ultimately, as Warren (1978) stresses, their success depends on the importance the organization attaches to selection and the quality of the training given.

Simulation of tasks that are entailed in the work candidates will be required to do, such as an 'in-basket' exercise in which individuals are required to deal with a series of memos such as they might find in their in-tray if in an executive role, are a feature of the extended interview and multiple assessment programmes used by a number of organizations to select and appraise their senior staff. Such programmes, which in Britain developed initially from officer-selection procedures in the armed forces and, subsequently, formed the basis of selection for the administrative class of the Civil Service, are now often referred to as 'assessment centres'. The term is associated particularly with managerial assessment procedures in large companies in the USA, pioneered by the American Telegraph and Telephone Company in 1956. The characteristic features of this 'multi-method, multi-trait, multi-assessor' approach are that people are assessed in groups: group exercises are a feature of the procedure. Often these include leaderless group discussions which are observed by a group or team of assessors who will also interview candidates individually and have available to them psychometric data and the results of other tests such as the 'in-basket' exercise and so on. It is a costly and lengthy procedure, but one which, if carefully controlled and monitored, has considerable advantages over single assessments based largely on interviews and general impressions of performance. As assessors usually comprise both senior managers and psychologists, the ultimate decision and report on any individual does not rest solely with either the professionals or line managers. However, much depends on how well lay assessors are trained in the techniques used, such as rating scales, interviewing, observation of specific behaviours, and their understanding of the dimensions of the total assessment. In industry, but not in the Civil Service or the armed forces, candidates attending assessment centres are usually given some feedback about their strengths and weaknesses, training needs and so on, which means that individuals as well as the organization may gain from these types of multiple assessment.

Training and development

The terms 'training', 'education', 'development' and 'learning', although not synonymous, are closely linked in definitions and descriptions of the means by which organizations seek to shape the behaviour of their members to achieve organizational objectives. Thus, the Department of Employment *Glossary of Training Terms* (1971) defines training as 'the systematic development of the attitude/knowledge/skill/behaviour pattern required by an individual to perform adequately a given task or job' and Hinrichs (1976) states that it may be defined as 'any organizationally initiated procedures which are intended to foster learning among organizational members in a direction contributing to organizational effectiveness'. Whereas 'training' refers to the formal and informal influences used to develop or modify people's attitudes, knowledge and skills, 'learning' denotes the process inferred to have taken place when behaviour and performance are observed to show enduring change as the result of experience.

Traditionally, education was distinguished from training in the sense that the former was associated with personal development and learning in academic institutions and training was seen in terms of a subsequent, once-and-for-all vocational training, that is as equipping someone with the necessary technical knowledge and skills to follow a particular occupation throughout his or her working life. Social and technological changes have made this model obsolete, given that the majority of careers are now likely to include some further education, up-dating, refresher courses, training and re-training in certain skills and the probability of discontinuous periods of employment. Rather than keeping the two concepts separate, therefore, it is more appropriate to regard education and training as complementary aspects of a single process of learning. Likewise, as all learning contributes to human development, the former distinction between 'training', in the sense of teaching people specific, job-related skills, and 'development', in the sense of helping them realize their overall potential, is also being eroded. Although the tendency persists to speak of managerial training as a largely developmental activity and to see operator training as primarily concerned with acquiring technical competence in a particular task, the need for flexibility and adaptability in the face of rapid and continuous changes in work and organizations has focused attention on the importance of attitude development and 'learning to learn' among all employees.

Since the end of the Second World War, organizations have invested more and more of their resources in training and development. Indeed, Porter *et al.* (1975), writing of the US scene, state that training costs are now one of the major financial costs incurred by organizations. In Britain, awareness of the need for a systematic, as opposed to an *ad hoc*, approach to training was reflected in the Industrial Training Act of 1964 and the Employment and Training Act of 1973, which were instrumental in stimulating widespread discussion and provision of training. Thomason (1981) suggests that this legislation was probably the outcome not only of changing conditions of employment, technological changes and production policies, which make it less and less likely that requisite work skills can be developed outside the work organization, but also of changing expectations on the part of employees as to what a good employer should provide. He points out that there is an increasing tendency for employers to recruit untrained people for jobs at the lower end of the undertaking's skill hierarchies and then, through training and development, to groom them to fill subsequent vacancies at higher levels, that is to rely more on the 'internal' than the 'external' labour market to meet their staffing requirements.

As psychologists have a long-standing interest in human development and learning, they might be expected to have made a significant contribution to training within organizations. However, their impact on practice has been limited in many instances because training is often undertaken by practitioners who are non-psychologists with strongly held beliefs about the efficacy of certain training methods and the inappropriateness of others. Furthermore, there is a dearth of comprehensive research directed towards solving training problems so that those who attempt an overview of psychological work in this field are often despondent or sharply critical in their comments. For example:

> Almost without exception, textbooks in Industrial and Organizational Psychology repeat the same tired list of 'principles' derived out of learning research when they deal with the topic of training – distribute practice, motivate the learner, make the learning task similar to the final task, etc. . . . Such principles, however, have been ignored by training practitioners with amazing regularity. (Hinrichs, 1976, p. 831)

Even if this is an unduly pessimistic view, there is no doubt that the efforts of organizations to teach new employees their jobs, to re-train existing staff in new techniques and to provide opportunities for education and self-development so as to enhance the career prospects of their members, are not necessarily effective or successful. From the point of view of the training practitioner, the main question is whether a particular training method works in a given context, that is whether it satisfies the organization concerned, rather than whether it extends knowledge of human learning. Consequently, training programmes are often built round the techniques with which the trainer is familiar and no attempt is made to discover how and why they are more effective than other methods of achieving the specific training objectives (Landy and Trumbo, 1980).

From an organizational perspective, the dimensions of training and development may be illustrated by table 2, which shows two distinct approaches espoused by trainers. The upper line, representing the view that what employees are taught and how they are to learn the requisite tasks and skills should be determined by

Table 2 Contrasting approaches to training

Policy	Strategy	Tactics	Evaluation
Performance and training objectives set by organization	Trainer-controlled, content-oriented teaching	Instruction and practice related to ultimate task performance	Achievement of target performance to required standards
Learner participates in setting own training and performance objectives	Experiential, self-directed, process-oriented learning	Removal of individual 'blocks' to learning	Increased sensitivity and continuing growth in self-awareness

the organization's trainers, embodies the traditional approach to learning, while the lower line reflects the belief that learning is an active process, accomplished most effectively when the individual participates in and takes responsibility for his or her learning. In theory, the two approaches are not necessarily incompatible, in the sense that one is directed primarily at specific accomplishments and technical performance and the other at enabling people to understand themselves better and thereby to realize their potential. However, in practice, trainers are apt to get 'boxed in' to one or other approach and, as indicated above, often confine themselves to employing a favourite or fashionable tactic (such as computer-assisted instruction or sensitivity training) which may not meet either the development policies of the organization or the expectations of the trainees. The latter permeate every cell of the table and have an important influence on the outcome of all types of training and educational programmes. For example, foremen anxious to know more about the technicalities of stock-control procedures, unit costs and budgeting, will be frustrated if the only training made available to them focuses on human relations and interpersonal skills. As one such group remarked, 'before we went on this course we suspected management was out of touch; now we *know* they are and it looks as it there is nothing we can do about it', a similar finding to that reported by Sykes (1962). Likewise, Schein (1965) points out that if new employees, when recruited, are promised challenging and meaningful jobs and then find themselves being trained for seemingly uninteresting tasks, they are likely to resist the training and become mistrustful of the organization as a whole.

Performance and control strategies

Recruitment, selection, training and development are all parts of the process by which organizations seek to attract, retain and motivate individuals to contribute consistently and effectively to the achievement of organizational objectives. Other aspects of the process include the setting and monitoring of performance standards, personnel policies and practices relating to pay, attendance and promotion, and the structuring and organization of work. As Blau and Schoenherr (1971) point out:

> An organization can be governed by recruiting anybody and everybody and then using a chain of command to rule them with an iron hand or installing a technology that harnesses them to machines. But an organization can also be managed by recruiting selectively only those employees that have the technical qualifications and professional interest to perform on their own the various tasks for which the organization is responsible. (Blau and Schoenherr, 1971, p. 16)

The approach adopted, according to Schein (1980), depends largely on the assumptions managers make about human behaviour and motivation. Organizations founded and run by those who believe that people cannot be trusted to work satisfactorily without close supervision and sanctions tend to use a system of tight controls, whereas organizations run by people who believe that their employees are motivated by inherently interesting jobs and opportunities for self-development in the work situation will devolve responsibility accordingly.

Awareness of the adverse psychological consequences for workers of the former view has increased in recent years, but there are signs of a new ideology developing to the effect that work is essential for personal development. This is a complicated issue to which we return in later chapters. While it would be wrong to believe that attempts to make work more agreeable to employees are necessarily manipulative, utilization of people's commitments to their work for control purposes may be 'insidious' according to

Blau and Schoenherr (1971), in the sense that its use as a controlling agent goes unrecognized.

The paradox that the greater the professionalization of an organization, the more closely bound to it the individual members become was noted by Burns and Stalker (1966) in their studies of manufacturing concerns in changing environments. As we discuss in the next chapter, the 'organic' systems of management they identified were adapted to unstable conditions. They entailed people yielding themselves as resources to be used by the work organization to a much greater extent than in traditional, hierarchically structured enterprises. Consequently employees were expected to have a 'professional' rather than a 'nine-to-five' orientation to their jobs with, in certain respects, a resulting loss of personal autonomy. Because everyone was 'in it together' in sustaining the enterprise, the sanctions applied the job performance derived more from this joint commitment and less from the formal contract of employment.

Regarding the appropriateness of high- or low-trust approaches to organization there is no 'one best way' to organize and manage an enterprise. The systems and procedures that prove effective are contingent on an organization's objectives, its technology and tasks, the people it employs and the environment in which it operates. For example, a manufacturing concern with two factories a few miles apart, producing the same products, was puzzled by the difference in response to an incentive payment system in the two plants until it took account of the differences in the age structure and domestic circumstances of their respective work-forces. In one, the majority of employees were setting up house and starting families, with the associated expenditure predisposing them to earn as much as possible, while in the other factory employees were older, had fewer dependents and many were waiting to be re-housed by the local authority. These factors therefore reinforced, but were not the direct cause of, contrasting group norms in the two plants, one centred on the acquisition of consumer goods which sanctioned high-bonus earnings as a short-term means to this end and the other based on keeping performance to a level judged comfortable by the group and within the limits of acceptability to management.

At all levels of an organization, the pattern and standards of behaviour expected, the limits of tolerance for deviation from the norm and the legitimacy of the authority exercised to encourage or enforce desired performance rest upon shared values and beliefs. Without some degree of consensus as to what is 'fair' and 'reasonable', whether in terms of effort, pay, attendance, management style, holiday entitlements, 'perks', accountability and responsibility, a topic of interest to social psychologists, no control strategy is likely to be effective and may be counter-productive. As Child (1977) observes, the traditional view of control as a process imposed from the apex of the organization downwards ignores the need to secure positive commitment and feedback from those at whom the control is directed.

Power and politics in organizations

Differences in organizations are rarely resolved by a naked exercise of power. However, it is undoubtedly true that the existence of power differentials and of different bases of power within organizations are highly significant for an understanding of behaviour within organizations. Power can be defined as a capacity to overcome resistance. Normally, however, differences are settled by the exercise of authority or through the processes of 'organizational politics'. 'Authority' is best understood as legitimized power, that is the exercise of a power which is *regarded as acceptable by those affected by it*. Authority is sustained as much by the expectations of those affected by its exercise as it is by any potential power an authority figure may be able to call upon to override any opposition. 'Organizational politics', on the other hand, refers to a wide range of influence-attempts that people engage in when important issues are at stake. 'Political' actions or decisions typically occur *when the addition of further information alone will not solve a particular problem.*

Identified in this way, it is evident that a wide range of behaviours can be dubbed 'political'. Personnel selection, for example, contains an element of organizational politics: people are chosen on the basis of evidence of their skills and achievements and also on hunches about such matters as how acceptable they are likely to be within the prevailing social ethos of an organization. More well recognized as examples of political behaviour in organizations are the preparing of agendas for committees, the ways information is presented to decision makers, and the tacit and subtle processes by which the premises upon which decisions are based become accepted by the decision makers themselves.

Organizational politics are perhaps most easily recognizable when temporary coalitions develop between different interest groups, when efforts are made to contain or co-opt dissenters to particular views, or when outside experts are selectively used to back the points of view of one faction.

It would be wrong to think that attempts to influence and control people in organizations are just the preserve of management. Although more senior members of an organization are well placed to influence their more junior colleagues, social control is not the exclusive province of senior managers. While they have different bases of power from which to direct their strategies, junior members of an organization can intervene very effectively in its political life. Junior staff can often frustrate attempts to impose unwelcome changes on them because of their detailed knowledge of operating conditions ('that wouldn't work because . . .'), their ability to make the changes seem more far reaching than they appear ('once you do this the consequences could be . . .') and by real or implied threats of general opposition. Moreover, a great deal of organizational politics takes place between people, not of different hierarchical levels, but from different functions or coalitions of functions. Such political behaviour within organizations is tantamount to bargaining behaviour and it may considerably modify the power relations formally prescribed by the organizational hierarchy.

As we discuss in the section on leadership in the next chapter there are a number of strategies that people can pursue to improve their individual political effectiveness within an organization. Two concepts, however, are particularly useful in analyzing the power structure of an organization. First, organizations are typically characterized by the presence of a *dominant ideology*. Within the general culture of Western industrialized countries, social values typically embrace such factors as economic rationality (where utilities and costs are compared and money is used as an indicator of value), economic growth (where national success is measured by indicators of economic expansion or of Gross National Product), technological development (through which human control is extended over the material world) and individualism (where personal worth is judged in terms of achievement, utility and thrift). Within many organizations it is hardly surprising, therefore, that a 'dominant ideology' can be identified where the values of rationality, progress and achievement find their expression in financial yardsticks of success. This obtains particularly in many private sector organizations. Within public sector organizations different dominant ideologies exist: universities, for example, cherish the values of truth and knowledge and hospitals the values of life and caring. While the relationship between the ways employees are assessed and an organization's dominant ideology is not always as clear as employees would sometimes like, the basis upon which judgements are made about people's performance, expertise and stature provide the clearest single indicator of the nature of the ideology that dominates within an organization.

Secondly, the concept of *dependencies* is of value in explaining structural bases of power. It has been suggested that the power one person has over another is equal to the dependence of the latter upon the former. An ability to provide needed resources or to cope with difficulties in an organization creates dependencies and enhances the power of one individual or group over another. Problems, as interpreted by the 'dominant ideology', will invariably develop to threaten an organization's effectiveness. The ability to cope with such difficulties becomes a key activity in an organization. Certain individuals and sub-units will find that, because of their functional role in the organization, it falls to them to deal with the problem. Success will breed success, as effective performance may lead to more resources being made available, so strengthening a unit's ability to deal with any future crisis. In this way the power of different functional groups in organizations can be explained. In British hospitals, perceptions of key problems identify doctors as the single most influential group, with nurses, administrators and auxiliary staff occupying far less prestigious positions. In business organizations the relative power of research and development, production or marketing departments will vary depending on particular circumstances: research, for example, is crucial in technologically advanced and developing industries such as pharmaceuticals; marketing is crucial for organizations operating in highly competitive markets for consumer goods such as cosmetics, confectionery or home computers. Within all private sector organizations, accountants and financial experts are normally accorded particular respect and, within most, personnel departments command relatively low prestige.

Power within organizations is therefore complex, manifesting itself not only in the actions of senior managers but also in the political activity of individuals and groups who are held in dif ferent degrees of respect. Psychologists have sometimes been accused of being 'soft on power' and of paying insufficient attention to its less obvious manifestations. However, as Pfeffer (1981) has noted, the analysis of power in organizations has been rather generally neglected. Primarily this has occurred because of the worrying issues that its study tends to raise. Before long in such an enquiry a distinctively *non*-rational element in the basis of existing power structures in organizations is likely to emerge. For example, just as control over the world's resources is distributed in a grossly uneven manner, so too control over strategic decision-making in large business organizations is normally the closely guarded province of a self-selecting elite. This contrasts markedly with claims for the efficiency, productivity and effectiveness of large organizations which, in the public mind, justify an unprecedented concentration of resources in modern organizations.

Discretion, trust and social exchange

It is usual to find a distinction between the terms and conditions of employment of jobs of different status within an organization as well as between those in different occupational categories – blue-collar, white-collar, professional, and so on. In general, the tighter the prescribed limits of work, such that a person can exercise very little discretion in his or her work role, the more likely is that person to be subject to close supervision, some form of payment by results, reprimands and penalties for lateness, absence and other externally imposed goals and sanctions. Conversely, the greater the discretionary element in a job, whereby an individual is responsible for the work done, with only limited reference to or review by an immediate superior, the more likely is that individual to be in a salaried, often highly paid position, with entitlements to 'fringe benefits' such as a company car, expense account, entertainment allowance or other status symbols. This contrast illustrates the ways in which the differing assumptions about human behaviour and motivation to which we referred earlier have become institutionalized. On the one hand, the view is that external sanctions and rewards are needed to get people to do what one wants them to do and, on the other, it is thought that reliance should be placed on self-control, self-managing units and internalized standards of 'professional' conduct. These contrasting types of work roles have been elaborated by Fox (1974) in discussing the differing degrees of trust embodied in the rules, roles and relationships governing people's behaviour in organizations. Table 3 shows the distinguishing features of what he terms the low-discretion syndrome and the high-discretion syndrome of patterns of work roles.

Although these represent the extremes of a continuum, which may apply to both vertical and lateral relationships, with many intermediate grades of medium discretion, they serve to highlight how low-discretion roles tend to generate low trust and a calculative exchange between the organization and the individual, whereas high-discretion roles incorporate and facilitate reciprocated trust. The key word here is 'tend', because low-discretion roles do not necessarily imply low-trust relationships or high-discretion roles high-trust relationships. Much depends on how

Table 3 Characteristics of low- and high-discretion work

Low-discretion work	High-discretion work
Perceived disposition of superordinates to behave as if role-occupant cannot be trusted	Superordinates assume personal commitment to organizational goals and/or to occupational calling by role-occupant
Close personal supervision, specific impersonal rules or other forms of systematic control	Freedom from close supervision and detailed regulation by specific impersonal rules
Tight co-ordination through externally applied standardized routines and schedules	Absence of standardized routines and emphasis on joint problem-solving
Communications in form of orders, commands, directions	Communications in forms of advice, information and consultative discussion
Failures or inadequate performance attributed to negligence or insubordination	Inadequate performances seen in terms of honest misjudgements or mistakes
Disagreements handled on basis of collective bargaining in the light of divergent goals	Disagreements handled on basis of 'working through' in light of shared goals

Fox (1974).

far those concerned are committed to the same or diverging goals and values. Furthermore, the structures and procedures that may encourage distrust at an institutional level do not mean that the same will apply at a personal level. As Fox puts it: 'The characteristic situation in industrial countries where collective bargaining is well developed is of confrontation between mutually suspicious hard bargainers who in personal terms respect, trust, and possibly even like each other' (Fox, 1974, p.105).

This perspective is rarely emphasized by those industrial and organizational psychologists who concentrate on what are assumed to be universal, individual motives and present the issue of the relationship between the organization and the individual largely in terms of the former providing the right inducements and incentives for the latter. Much of the prescriptive writing on managerial strategies aimed at increasing workers' attachment to their work and their identification with organizational objectives either ignores the industrial-relations context or is at too high a level of abstraction to apply in a specific situation.

Take, for example, the issue of absenteeism which occurs widely in low-discretion work and which is generally perceived as a form of individual rather than social behaviour. From a managerial perspective, persistent absentees are 'work-shy', unreliable employees whose behaviour needs to be corrected by various sanctions. Social scientists and medical officers, on the other hand, are apt to regard it as a symptom of, or response to, stress or adverse working conditions and seek to remedy the situation by alleviating the presumed cause, for instance by re-designing people's jobs or by individual counselling. However, extensive research by Chadwick-Jones et al. (1982) showed that there are distinctive patterns of absence discernible within given organizations and occupations, suggesting that absences should be seen as part of the social exchange between managers and employees. In other words, in a specific environment there is usually a tacit understanding between managers, supervisors and workers about the nature of this exchange, such as whether absence may be traded off against excessively tight work schedules, and collusive agreement as to what levels of absence are acceptable.

'Employees' motivations to come to work operate within a context that to a large extent predetermines how much absence the individual will take, how often and when. Even more important, this context of employee–employer organizational relationships will influence the extent to which absence is available as an option, and certainly the limits to which it is available and the particular forms it will take: sickness, non-sickness, medium-duration or short-term. (Chadwick-Jones *et al.*, 1982, p.16)

In their view, any long-term change in prevailing patterns of absence behaviour, which are extremely costly to management, will only come about by 're-negotiating the norm' with the groups concerned and not by measures aimed at the individual employee (e.g. attendance bonuses for absence-free periods at work) which will, at best, have only a short-term effect.

This proposition appeared self-evident to a student from a northern ship-building town where the sense of occupational community remains strong, despite the decline of the industry. She was surprised and indignant to discover how absenteeism has been variously interpreted as an index of morale, alienation or irresponsible attitudes to work. 'Where I come from,' she said, 'there's no question of which comes first if the local team's playing at home or a friend's getting married and it clashes with work, you support your mates and management understands they must put up with it.' She then added reflectively, 'I suppose if I were a bank manager's daughter from the home counties and had been brought up on the work ethic, I'd think differently', comments which illustrate the social dimensions of the problem.

It is not, therefore, solely a matter of what goes on within organizations that determines people's attachments to work and their loyalties and allegiances. Prior socialization as to what is regarded as 'normal' behaviour in a given environment precludes any success in seeking an organizational formula that can be applied universally. Behaviour in organizations is behaviour within a social context and cannot be considered adequately without taking account of these social influences.

4

Organizational processes and structure

As a society, we have become increasingly
aware of the fact that we live, work and
play in multi-cultural surroundings.
Moreover . . . it is becoming clear that the
origins of many of these cultures are not
coupled conceptually to matters such as
geography, ethnicity or social class, but are
grounded in organizational experiences.
Whether we are examining the
organizational worlds of middle managers,
tramps, stockbrokers, high-school
principals, police officers, production
workers or professional crooks, we are
certain to uncover special languages,
unique and peculiar problems, and, more
generally, distinct patterns of thought and
action.   (Van Maanen, 1979, p. 522)

Social influences in organizations

Attempts to influence and control people, be these overt or covert,
are a key aspect of organizational life. The very nature of organizations makes this inevitable. If people are to co-operate in the
pursuit of a common goal, objectives and sub-objectives need to

be specified, a division of labour has to be made and people need to assume differentiated roles and accept responsibility for separate tasks. Yet organizations only rarely work in quite the ways in which they have been designed. The size and complexity of modern organizations are such that they compound the competing and collaborative relationships that engage their members. Moreover, different interest groups emerge in organizations, with disagreements arising between them over such matters as priority goals and appropriate methods by which such goals may be achieved. In this chapter, we consider some psychological contributions to our understanding of organizational dynamics, first in terms of group processes and then in relation to leadership, both of which have to be seen in the wider context of organizational structures.

Groups within organizations

Although they have been subjected to severe criticism on methodological grounds, the 'Hawthorne studies' by Mayo and his associates in the inter-war years (see chapter 1), showed how group norms could affect output. Their impact, together with that of the research and theory developed by Lewin (1947) and others on group dynamics, has led a number of theorists to suggest that groups are the 'building blocks' of organizations, the effect of group membership on individual behaviour being the key to effective task accomplishment and worker satisfaction.

This view rests on the concept of a psychological group, defined by Schein (1980) as 'any number of people who (1) interact with one another, (2) are psychologically aware of one another, and (3) perceive them themselves to be a group' (p. 145). The basic notion, as Sprott (1958) explains, is relatively exclusive interaction in a given context:

> You would say that the people working in a factory form a group because, in the context of their occupation, they interact with one another more than they interact with other people, so far as their occupation goes. Within the factory, men or women co-operating in a special job form a group – a subgroup with respect to the factory as a whole – for the same reason. (Sprott, 1958, p. 9)

In terms of organizational processes, it is these smaller, formal task groups, set up on either a permanent (e.g. the accounts department) or temporary basis (e.g. a salary-review committee) which are crucial to management in seeking to achieve organizational goals. They are also important to employees in providing the opportunity for face-to-face contact with others, companionship, recognition by peers of their technical and social skills, and so on. Over and above these formal groups, however, are the informal groups which arise spontaneously out of shared interests, off-the-job contacts (e.g. travelling on the same bus or train to work) and other affiliations. These exist within and across the formally constituted task groups and may be facilitated or inhibited by factors such as the location of departments and offices, time and work schedules, car-parking allocations and the like. The greater the frequency of informal meetings that take place between people in their normal day-to-day activities, the greater the likelihood of their forming an informal group, even of a tenuous nature. Like formal groups, informal groups may be enduring or of short-term duration, as when individuals form a temporary coalition to further their own ends and/or frustrate those of others. In short, as Schein (1980) puts it:

> Groups of all kinds will always be found in organizations, some formal ones created by deliberate design to do specific jobs, some informal ones created by the needs of people to interact, and some which form simply because of the probability of interaction created by physical proximity, similarity of interests, or other fortuitous factors. (Schein, 1980, p. 149)

The functions of groups and effective group functioning

Both experimental and field studies of groups show that they fulfil a number of functions which may be categorized broadly under two headings. These are *the psychological rewards* of membership for individuals and *the instrumental functions* of groups for organizations.

Regarding the first of these, groups are extremely significant in people's lives. They provide important sources of support in developing and maintaining a person's sense of identity and esteem; they are an outlet for affiliation needs; they are a means of establishing and testing social reality through shared perceptions and interpretations of social events; they reduce the uncertainty, anxiety or sense of powerlessness experienced in ambiguous or threatening situations; and they may enable people to realize personal objectives requiring corporate action. Not all groups fulfil all these functions, but such a list shows why people usually feel stronger and more comfortable as members of a group than they do in isolation, which is why 'being sent to Coventry' is such a powerful sanction and solitary confinement so hard to endure.

Indeed, the importance of the psychological functions that groups fill has been dramatically illustrated by the experiences of people who have been systematically denied the supports that they normally provide. During the early years after the Second World War, reports of the confessions of apparently innocent individuals in the purge trials held in Eastern bloc countries led many westerners to believe that techniques for brainwashing had been developed in the communist countries. Fears that people's individuality could be usurped by the implantation of a pre-programmed package of behavioural responses were reinforced by the apparent defections of US servicemen captured during the Korean war. Experts in the USA, therefore, began an anxious search for the *deus ex machina*, to discover whether it was by drugs, hypnosis, ultrasonics, lobotomy or some other means that such effects had been achieved.

Later analysis of what happened in Korea indicated that those unlikely confessions, defections and changes of allegiance which had taken place could be attributed, not to a new technique of drug control or the like, but to the combined effects of techniques of individual disorientation and group fragmentation. Following the shock of defeat and capture, uniforms had been removed from the US servicemen, little food provided, resistance had been threatened by death and the prisoners marched for several days with no help allowed for the sick or wounded. In the camps, ranks had been segregated, people's attempts to organize broken up, mistrust had been fostered, and it was made clear that spies were operating in the camps. Religious expression was banned and news from outside was unavailable. Extensive interrogation of the prisoners took place. The inmates were exposed to lengthy and persistent programmes of propaganda. Following lectures, for example, in which novel interpretations of the causes of the war were provided, people were required to 'discuss' their content in an approved manner and, if they would not, to attend the lecture again until they were so prepared. As informal groups emerged, supportive of people's resistance, they were systematically broken up. Thus, experiences of profound disorientation, disillusionment and absence of group support were engineered. A person's sense of identity had been attacked, feelings of guilt and betrayal encouraged, conflict and fear fostered, peer-group supports undermined. At this point escape routes were offered in the guise of new rationalizations and behaviours. Signs of leniency were presented with apparent opportunities for relief from the pressure. Compulsions to 'confess' sometimes developed which, when exploited, could lead to the person submitting and attributing guilt to the persona of his past and to the system of which he had been a product.

It should be noted that only a minority of people subjected to this process of 'brainwashing' internalized the propaganda fed to them, although a degree of compliance was a common reaction. People's sense of identity is not solely dependent on group support, as personality structures are clearly of significance. However, the social roles we adopt and are accepted in are of great importance to us all. As far as the Korean POW's were concerned, once re-united with family, friends and re-integrated into normal social relationships, although not unscarred by the brutality of their experiences, most re-adjusted their lives successfully. The experiences they had suffered showed clearly how groups help people to function adequately as individuals. Although the example of brainwashing is an extreme one its implications for more normal circumstances are clear: individuality and sociability should not be thought of as opposites because, as we showed in chapter 2, it is through our membership of various groups that we develop a mature sense of our own identities.

In addition to the psychological functions that groups fulfil, groups in organizations serve a number of instrumental functions. These have been listed by Handy (1976) as including: the distribution of work; the management and control of work; information processing; data collection; problem-solving and decision-making; liaison and co-ordination; negotiation or conflict resolution; socialization and training of employees; and other task-related activities. In other words, it is largely in and through groups that managers seek to achieve expected standards of performance and to promote organizational effectiveness. The latter will only be accomplished, many theorists argue, if task groups are designed so as to fulfil the personal functions outlined above, that is to structure work groups so that they are psychologically satisfying to their members.

In considering the conditions under which cohesive and committed task groups emerge within organizations it is evident that a wide range of significant factors is relevant. These include: the intrinsic interest of a group's task (if the task is interesting cohesion tends to be higher); the extent to which group members need to depend on each other (greater mutual dependencies facilitate greater cohesion); and the attractiveness of the broader organization to the group members (if they are proud to be members of the organization group members may be more strongly attracted to the group). Considerable importance, however, must be attached to the patterns of interaction among group members themselves. *Task related* behaviours are easily recognized in groups; they include the setting of objectives, defining and allocating tasks and roles, the development of ideas, the provision of information and evaluation of progress. *Group maintenance* behaviours are, while less immediately obvious, none the less significant for an understanding of what is happening in a group. How people are interacting, whether they trust each other, and the ways feelings can acceptably be expressed in the group are crucially important issues for the effective functioning of a group as Bales (1951), for example, demonstrates in his classic studies of group processes. Dominating or obstructive behaviours can be highly dysfunctional. As a rule of thumb, just as a group needs people who will fulfil task roles and act as initiators, so too it needs people who will help reconcile disagreements, keep communication channels open and facilitate participation, test for consensus, encourage and confront others, and evaluate the quality of the group's processes. Effectiveness in group-maintenance behaviours is as important to the long-term success of a group as the short-term achievement of particular goals. Resentment, lack of involvement, dependence, conformity and mistrust are the common results of insufficient skills being exercised in this area.

An example of the importance of maintenance behaviours is provided by people's reactions when they first join a new group. Interpersonal interactions are particularly significant to the new member as he or she attempts to discover the actual or developing norms of the group. How open or formal people are in the group, how sympathetic or supportive, who are the most influential members of the group and what roles a newcomer is expected or permitted to assume are all matters of some significance. To try and understand the situation, the new member will be particularly attentive to matters such as who leads discussion and what is discussed, who interrupts whom, who is ignored, the style of interaction within the group, and the many non-verbal messages people convey through patterns of eye contact, seating arrangements, bodily movements and so on.

The significance of these behaviours raises another issue central to an understanding of group processes. This is the question of group conformity and the extent to which group members can become vulnerable to pressures which, far from being liberating, result in their acting in ways to which they would not otherwise be inclined. Given the range of functions that groups serve in people's lives, it is safe to predict that informal groups with identifiable norms will inevitably emerge in organizations. But where willing participation in group norms ends, and more passive conformity to them begins, is a difficult question. Norms are best understood as a summary of the influence processes operating in a group. They develop slowly and are concerned with behaviours significant to group members. Not all norms apply to everyone, because roles become differentiated, with some variations developing in the characteristic behaviours that are expected of different group members. What can be said is that while some people are undoubtedly more susceptible to group pressures than others, as a general rule, people are more likely to conform to pressures they are uncertain about if they hold the members of the group in high esteem and if they rate the group's ability to meet their own needs very highly.

Pressures to conform in groups responsible for decision-making can, if allowed to develop, lead to disastrous consequences. An example of this is provided by Janis' (1972) informative descriptions of recent foreign policy fiascos in which US governments have been involved. One example he discusses is President Kennedy's handling of the 'Bay of Pigs' invasion of Cuba, comparing this to his far more successful handling of the Cuban missile crisis. The former occurred very soon after Kennedy assumed office in 1961, when he allowed CIA plans for the invasion of Cuba by Cuban exiles to proceed with the aid of the US Air Force and Navy. Within three days this episode ended in disaster (Janis describes it as a 'perfect failure' with most of the invaders captured or killed by Castro's soldiers). The Cuban missile crisis occurred only some 18 months later. But in this case Kennedy's successful diplomacy and blockade of Soviet ships led to agreement that missile sites then being assembled on Cuban soil should be dismantled and the threat of world war was avoided.

Reviewing the evidence of how decisions were reached during these difficult periods, Janis identified the phenomenon of 'groupthink', a term he coined with the 'newspeak' vocabulary of George Orwell's *1984* very much in mind. 'Groupthink' occurs when groups under stress engage in concurrence-seeking behaviour at the expense of engaging with their task problems. The group's ability to make judgements and evaluate reality is lost as members reassure themselves by not considering the possibility of error. Few courses of action are considered in such groups, the one chosen is not later reviewed, outside experts are not consulted, and no contingency plans are prepared. An illusion of invulnerability developed in Kennedy's cabinet before the 'Bay of Pigs' fiasco, as an atmosphere of assumed consensus developed. Interestingly, it was the same individuals who were in Kennedy's cabinet during the 'Bay of Pigs' invasion who helped him avert the potential holocaust threatened by the Cuban missile crisis. But, during this period, a different group norm was cultivated. Pet ideas were reviewed and demolished in cabinet. The reality of the dangers of the situation were emphasized, moral issues were explicitly discussed, and cabinet members openly changed their minds. Although in times of stress 'groupthink' seems quite likely to occur among decision makers (for example, it has been suggested that during the Falklands crisis groupthink developed in the Thatcher cabinet), the general message of Janis' analysis is an optimistic one. While group pressures towards conformity can be considerable, group norms are not unchangeable and significant developments are possible in the roles that people enact in their groups.

Myths of leadership

The topic of leadership invokes an aura of romance and mythology that is deeply ingrained in our culture. Great things are expected of effective leaders. The heroic images of a Kennedy or a Napoleon, Churchill or Mao Tse-Tung provide emotive models that are, in the public mind, often equated with leadership in general. 'Here was a Caesar! When comes such another?' proclaims Mark Antony in Shakespeare's *Julius Caesar*. The potency of the popular image of impressive leaders has meant that too much is generally expected of the phenomenon of 'leadership' and, until recently, psychologists have tended to adopt rather simplistic assumptions about it.

In introducing this topic, therefore, it is helpful to identify a number of prevalent misunderstandings. Four myths of leadership should be noted. The *first myth* is that *leaders are invariably very important*. The reality of the experience of many who occupy formal leadership roles is that they often feel surprisingly frustrated and ineffectual in their roles. From where their subordinates stand it may seem that their bosses are well placed to make things happen. But people's tendencies to attribute significance in this way is often quite wrong; managers frequently find that the very most they can hope to do is to ride the tide of events in which they are involved, as to control them is an impossibility. Studies of how leaders in work organizations spend their time show that, typically, they are involved in a large number of different activities throughout their working day, need to react quickly to a variety of demands and exert very little immediate strategic control over the matters coming before them.

The *second myth* is the belief that *effective leaders have particular personality characteristics*. Practically every desirable human characteristic has been said to be associated with effective leadership: vigour, intelligence, originality, stability, good judgement, determination, persistence. But this approach is *very* misleading. It is difficult to define these traits with any precision, their relationship to particular acts of leadership is obscure and, above all, there is *no* convincing evidence that the stereotype vision of the confident extrovert leader has any relationship to actual leadership behaviour in many situations.

While attempts to chart the relationship between personality and effective leadership have generally proved very disappointing, it is important to note that, given the strength of popular imagery in this area, the approach is still very appealing to a great many non-psychologists. The myth surfaces in many ways. In 1974 a number of senior British industrialists signed the following advertisement:

> So far as we are concerned three years as an Army Officer can equal three years at University.

53

Of course, we don't expect a young man fresh from the Army to be fluent in Medieval French Literature or a Master of Microbiology.

But in our experiences as employers, we've found that a Short Service Commission in the Army equips a man to make the change to business management very easily.

For both jobs are concerned with the handling of people and getting the best out of them, often in trying situations.

(Anyone who's had to keep twenty soldiers calm when a crowd is hurling bricks at them will readily agree). . . .

And to be frank, there's another aspect we like. All managers have to learn the hard way, and this will have been at the Army's expense, not ours. (*The Times*, 16 June 1974)

The signatories to this statement clearly believed that a person's suitability for a leadership role in civilian organizations was enhanced by the character-developing experiences provided by a short service army commission. The stereotype of a coolly efficient army machine may be an attractive organizational model for 'captains of industry' to aspire to. However, it is not at all clear that the allegedly character-developing experiences of handling men in the army, a services' view of teamwork and the army emphasis on following orders with energy provide a particularly good basis for leadership behaviour in other, non-military, contexts. In non-military organizations the bases of influence and authority are likely to be very different from those available to military personnel, as are the expectations people have of their leaders, the structures within which leaders have to operate and the very tasks they have to perform. The idea that an individual 'matured' by his or her experiences in one leadership situation will prove to be a suitable leader in quite another is naïve and it seems unhelpful to compare the suitability of army officers and university graduates for management positions in the way attempted in the advertisement. One reason why the 'character-trait theory' of leadership continues to flourish, despite its poor basis in evidence, is that, for people in senior positions, and possibly for others also, it is comforting to believe that leaders have achieved their success by virtue of their superior personal qualities.

The *third myth* is the assumption that *particular leadership styles are invariably more effective than others*. As a reaction against the suggestion that different character traits distinguish good and bad leaders, attempts have been made to describe different ways in which leaders approach their tasks. Two theories rose to prominence in the late 1960s, both identifying particular styles as, allegedly, the most appropriate ones for leaders to adopt. One theory classified leader styles by the extent to which a leader engages in 'consideration' behaviour and in behaviour classified as 'initiating structure'. This classification reflects the distinction between 'group maintenance' and 'task' behaviours that we discussed earlier. Thus 'consideration' refers to the extent to which a leader's behaviour indicates consideration of his or her subordinates' needs, a preparedness to explain his or her point of view, and a generally sympathetic and friendly outlook. 'Initiating structure' is, on the other hand, not concerned with employee-orientation, but with production-centred behaviours. It refers to the extent to which a leader emphasizes work goals, methods and achievements. These two separate dimensions can be used to distinguish different styles (e.g. high consideration, low structure and high structure, low consideration). Popularized by Blake and Mouton (1964) this approach has been adopted widely in training courses; managers are asked to explore their own and others' perceptions of their leader styles and to experiment with the style reckoned to be superior, that is the high consideration, high initiating-structure style.

The second popular theory of an 'ideal' leader style was advocated by Likert (1961), who suggested that leader styles could be arranged along a continuum ranging from autocracy through benevolent autocracy and consultative leadership, to a participative approach. Likert's own approach was to use evidence from a wide variety of studies to argue that participative approaches were the most likely to be associated with high productivity, facilitating as they may high degrees of group loyalty, effective interpersonal interaction and commitment to high performance goals.

Although these contributions were undoubtedly an advance on what had gone before, the claim that particular styles are *invariably* superior is not easy to square with the evidence. The complexity of leadership has been illustrated by studies which show that, despite a general preference for participative leadership, some people do prefer authoritarian leaders; that it is not easy to act in a participative way when one is working in a generally authoritarian organization; that consistency in style may be more important for subordinate satisfaction than the style itself (people like to know what to expect of their leaders); and that the nature of people's tasks constrains the leadership role (with routine assembly-line work, for example, requiring more courteous first-line supervision than craft work, where general technical support skills are likely to be in greater demand). Moreover, group problem-solving may have risks: as our discussion of 'groupthink' illustrated, social pressures can distort people's judgements; individuals within groups can come to dominate them; and 'just winning' an argument may emerge as a major target for individuals in a competitive group atmosphere. In short, just as a search for universal leadership traits failed, so has the search for universally effective leader styles. To a significant extent, appropriate leader styles are, it would appear, situationally dependent.

The *fourth myth* of leadership has been one reaction to these very insights: it is the idea that *simple 'contingency' models can be devised* to guide people towards an appropriate leadership style. One such theory has been developed by Vroom (1976). It endeavours to distinguish situations in which unilateral decisions by a leader are likely to be more effective than those in which a participative approach would be appropriate. Depending on answers to various questions concerned with the necessary quality of the particular decision that has to be made, and the necessity for it to be accepted by group members, allegedly appropriate decision-making styles for particular situations are suggested. Used as a training device, Vroom hoped that this algorithmic model could help leaders develop a sensitivity to conditions when they should adopt different behavioural styles.

At first sight, theories such as this have an apparent sophistication, promising as they do to solve the enigma of leader effectiveness. But it is doubtful if it is realistic to hope that they can be very successful in this. Basic to their approach is the idea that the leadership situation is composed of a small number of fixed dimensions. But the relevant parameters of one situation are unlikely to be the same elsewhere, and it is unwise to adopt a prescriptive orientation in the absence of detailed knowledge about any particular situation. Moreover, theories like this take a surprisingly mechanistic approach to group dynamics. What happens over time is a key issue in leadership. Over a period, unilateral styles of decision-making have undesirable results. Group members tend to become detached or resentful. They will not have had the opportunity to learn the skills of decision-making that a shared approach to leadership would have encouraged. They may show little inclination to become more involved.

Leadership and group effectiveness

The study of leadership is, therefore, a complex matter, often overrated in importance, surrounded by popular misunderstandings and characterized by attempts to develop simplistic theories of 'how to do it'. None the less, there are a number of observations that can be made to clarify the situation somewhat.

Leadership style is, as we discuss below, a significant issue and its relevance to effective group processes should not be underestimated. Yet, for formally appointed leaders in organizations, it is only one aspect of a complex of interrelated factors. The manager's job requires skills that include, but are broader than, the skills of leadership as traditionally defined. A manager may only spend a small proportion of the working day with his or her subordinates. Skills of communication, memory and a tolerance for the many different tasks they have to become involved in are important ingredients of managerial success.

One important service performed by theories of leadership style, however, has been to draw attention to the effectiveness of alternative bases for influence than those leaders acquire by virtue of their appointed positions alone. French and Raven (1967) distinguish between a number of possible bases of authority that leaders can call upon. Formally appointed leaders have certain powers to administer rewards and punishments. By virtue of their special status in the hierarchy their wishes normally command a legitimacy that others cannot call upon. These bases of authority are well understood and, traditionally, managers are expected to rely upon them. Yet, as French and Raven argue, leaders can also acquire influence with their subordinates if they are seen to be expert in their jobs and if they can become effective in their interpersonal relationships. Theories of participative leader styles and of 'initiating structure' and 'consideration' emphasize the importance of these observations and point towards the dangers of too heavy a reliance on the formal attributes of position and status.

What should also be emphasized is the fact that participative leadership requires social skills of a high order. It is wrong to

57

believe that all participation requires is for the leader to step back and 'let the group sort it out'. As Maier (1970) points out, participation requires a very active leader who: effectively shares information with others; prevents dominant individuals dominating the proceedings; helps to involve the more reticent; helps people communicate effectively; prevents deviant ideas from a premature rejection; re-directs unfocused discussion; encourages fresh analysis; and guides the process of screening alternatives and selecting solutions. Interestingly, such behaviours in a leader go some way to preventing tendencies towards 'groupthink', as they legitimize the articulation of differences and the mutual exploration of new ideas. But the skills needed to do this well are not easy to acquire. It may be that the single most important barrier to a more general use of collaboration is the fact that the behavioural styles which people commonly adopt in organizations are neither very participative in themselves nor create the conditions necessary for leaders to learn to become more participative.

One theory of action developed by Argyris (1976) examines why this is so. Argyris points out that the 'espoused' theories that people hold about action (i.e. what they say they believe), are often at variance with their 'theories in use' (i.e. what appears to guide their actual behaviour). Because people state that participation is their preferred approach, this does not guarantee that, in practice, they will act participatively. Argyris does not suggest this is because of hypocrisy; indeed he feels people can become very frustrated when they realize how unsuccessful they are in their efforts to be collaborative. He suggests, however, that people are socialized to seek to control their social interactions, to emphasize purpose and rationality in disregard of others' feelings. Moreover, as people seek to control others, they will tend to receive little feedback on the effects their behaviour is having on those they are seeking to influence. People quickly learn that, despite any lip-service to the contrary, it is competition and not collaboration which is the name of the game. As a result, an atmosphere of caution develops which reinforces the leader's implicit suspicion that control is needed in interpersonal relationships.

Argyris recommends the values of informed, free and committed group decision-making as an alternative approach. In behavioural terms, leaders need to combine an advocacy of their own views with a respect for others' opinions and an open enquiry about their suitability. Outcomes of such an approach include progressive learning by the leader and by group members, the possibility of substantial revisions of decision premises and the avoidance of self-fulfilling prophesies in leadership. Argyris' theory suggests that leaders should be less concerned to achieve particular outcomes and more concerned about the decision-making processes they utilize. As he points out, the difficulties people face in moving from a controlling orientation over their colleagues towards a genuinely collaborative approach are not to be underestimated.

Finally, it should be noted that leaders in organizations often have important functions to play in representing their group's views to other individuals and groups within the broader organization, to which they can take a number of approaches. Pettigrew's (1976) analysis, from a sociological perspective, of possible tactics that people can use to gain influence with their own bosses has helped to illuminate some of the processes involved. The *access* that people cultivate with significant people in the organization is one key factor. Such access will partly be a function of work roles and hierarchical positions, but considerable latitude for developing access beyond the functional minimum normally exists. It has been argued that the greater the variety of contacts a person develops with influential others, the easier it is for that person to develop relationships that can be beneficial. Contacts through special project work, social contacts within work or shared sports and spare-time activities outside it may all be useful. Access in itself, however, only provides a person with the opportunity to develop helpful social relationships. His or her *assessed stature* is crucial in making use of the contacts he or she has. Importantly his or her credibility and trustworthiness will be judged by the interpersonal impact he or she makes and by the extent to which he or she becomes accepted as a valued 'insider' in tune with appropriate priorities and ideologies. Other key factors in developing a position of influence include, of course, a person's perceived *expertise*, in particular his or her 'track record' in present and past jobs and the relevance of his or her special skills and achievements for other people's priority needs. And an additional factor of importance is the control a person may acquire over *information* that others find useful in their activities. Pettigrew's list emphasizes the political dimension of the leadership role. Leaders who, on behalf of their groups, are effective in influencing key personnel elsewhere in the organization will normally

59

find that their prestige in their own group will be considerably enhanced.

Organization structures and effectiveness

At the start of this chapter we made brief reference to the processes by which organizations are formally structured: objectives and sub-objectives are formulated, a division of labour is effected, people are held responsible for the performance of their separate tasks. The term 'organizational structure' refers to the generally fixed relationships that exist among the members of an organization including, for example, job definitions, the delineation of units or departments and the lines of authority in the organization. Structural factors such as these attract a lot of attention in the management literature as it is through the formal design of an organization that managers endeavour to control and co-ordinate its activities.

Basic to an understanding of the structuring of organizations is the concept of 'bureaucracy'. As it is commonly used nowadays the term has connotations of red-tape and inefficiency and is frequently used pejoratively in critical reference to public sector organizations or to large unresponsive institutions. However, in the history of the modern state the bureaucratic form of organization has a special place as it has facilitated an unprecedentedly high degree of organizational effectiveness. As originally analysed by Weber (1947), procedures are defined in clear terms in a bureaucracy, a division of labour is effected and abstract rules govern the operations of the organization; employees are hired on the basis of their technical qualifications for their work, are required to conduct their affairs in an impersonal way and are protected from arbitrary dismissal. Accordingly, despite the poor popular image of bureaucracies in the public mind, their potential for effective functioning should not be underestimated. Rules do not necessarily mean red-tape, as bad rules may be conspicuous but good rules are hardly noticed. Areas of discretion can be delineated by rules and, as they will be derived from past experience, they can help ensure consistency, efficacy and fairness. Moreover, an important aspect of bureaucracies is the expectation that employees should not act in their own selfish interests or exploit the opportunities for nepotism that their membership of the organization might provide.

To some extent, through their procedural rules and routines and their division into specialized functions and hierarchical divisions, all modern organizations show elements of bureaucratization. But in recent years it has been recognized increasingly that the bureaucratic concept is inherently limited. Psychological theory points to the limitations of too much reliance on reward, punishment and legitimate bases of authority. The significance of groups and the motivating potential of cohesive work-oriented groups can go unrecognized in bureaucratic organizations. The benefits of interesting and responsible work can be overlooked as few decisions are permitted at the lower levels of bureaucracies. Communications tend to pass downwards, but less frequently pass up the hierarchy. Apathy at junior grades and mistrust between junior and senior levels tends to be the norm in bureaucracies; people in senior positions often come to believe that there is no alternative to employing strict controls over more junior personnel. To the extent, therefore, that the bureaucratic form of organization limits discretion, fosters mistrust, underestimates the potential of groups to be self-regulative and relies too heavily on rationality and formal authority as guides to action, it is based on a poor understanding of individual and social psychology.

Bureaucracies are notoriously slow to react to changing conditions. Within them it is the officials at the top of the hierarchy who control the organization's relationships with the outside world. Their perception of priorities and the perceptions of their juniors can quickly become segmented. For middle and junior personnel a role orientation can easily develop where the objectives of different procedures can become lost in a defence of the procedures themselves. Similarly, different functional groups in a bureaucracy can easily come to pursue their own priorities in disregard of the broader needs of their organization. Bureaucratic organization structures are built around the premise that a clarity of objectives in the organization is possible and that the acceptability of senior managers' rulings on priorities will go unquestioned. Today, when many organizations face rapidly changing circumstances, serve a variety of needs for several interest groups and cannot depend so readily on the accepted legitimacy of senior officials, such assumptions are often untenable. In table 4 a number of key organizational problems are listed, with the suitability of the traditional solutions that are embedded in bureaucratic structures compared to present-day circumstances. These

Table 4 Key organizational issues and the suitability of bureaucratic organizational structures.

Key issues	Traditional solutions and their current suitability	
(1) How *adaptable* should the organization be?	Bureaucracies are well suited to stable environments and to making routine responses to them	The environments of many modern organizations are fast changing and uncontrollable by the organization
(2) What are the *goals* of the organization?	A consistency and clarity of organizational purpose is assumed in a bureaucracy	The priorities of many modern organizations are multiple and complex, fluctuating and controversial
(3) What are *the bases of authority* that officials in the organization depend upon?	Rationality and legality are emphasized in bureaucracies, through reward, punishment and legitimate authority	Traditional views on the legitimacy of 'management prerogatives' have significantly changed in recent years; new, participative approaches to leadership are generally expected
(4) How are *differences resolved* within the organization?	Within bureaucracies the different priorities of sub-groups are resolved by rules or by more senior officials within the hierarchy	The long-term problems of relying on authority figures to resolve differences is becoming better understood; where complex interdependencies exist a collaborative approach to problem-solving is beneficial
(5) How is *effort integrated* within the organization?	In bureaucracies tasks are differentiated; value is placed on a role orientation and on a loyalty to the organization as a whole	The benefits to productivity and satisfaction of interesting and responsible work have been well documented and are now quite widely recognized

indicate why there is widespread interest in developing alternatives to bureaucracies, developments to which psychologists, sociologists and management theorists are all making important contributions.

One such alternative emerged from the studies by Trist (1981) and others at the Tavistock Institute of Human Relations of the introduction of mechanized methods of coal mining in Britain in the 1950s and early 1960s. The old method of mining involved small, self-selecting teams of about three people working together at the coal-face. The miners in each team combined to cut the coal, move it, fix roof supports in place and were paid a common wage packet. Trist and his colleagues described how a semi-automatic mechanized system of coal cutting (the Longwall method) allowed the Coal Board to introduce a new system where an extensive area of coal-face could be worked at one time by large groups paced by the machinery. In one mine forty to fifty men worked for an eight-hour shift on small parts of the overall operation, with different functional groups being paid separately. The new system necessitated far greater emphasis on supervision than had previously been needed. As researchers noted, absence and accident rates were high under the new fragmented work system, the morale of the miners was greatly reduced and poor relations developed between the shifts. Later a mine in Durham was studied where, although the same mechanization equipment had been installed, a different organizational system had been developed around it. Multi-skilled teams had been created with the men rotated around the shifts and payment made to each shift as a whole. Production figures, absenteeism and indicators of morale all showed that this method, known as the Composite Longwall system, was a considerable improvement on the conventional Longwall method.

These studies were to provide many of the insights that were later developed into 'socio-technical systems' theory. As we discuss in chapter 7, they drew attention to the importance of technological and structural factors in explanations of people's behaviour in organizations. Trist and his colleagues were to propose that, while technologies influence organizational structures in an important way, a wide range of possible methods for their integration can often be found. On this view social and psychological factors should be given an equal weight to technological ones. From their understanding of behavioural factors the

Table 5 Key organizational issues and alternative structural arrangements.

Key issues	Bureaucracies	Autonomous workgroups	Organic structures
(1) *Organizational adaptability*	Stable and predictable environment is assumed; a strong role orientation limits internal flexibility	High internal flexibility of means; strong feelings of loyalty to colleagues and to the group's task may limit flexibility of aims	Open communications encourage receptivity to changes in means and aims; such change is possible without requiring changes to structure, which is fluid; strong task- and progress-oriented norms
(2) *Organizational goals*	Consistency and clarity of purposes is assumed	Consistency of aims is assumed, but people's capacity for learning is higher than in a bureaucracy	Continual re-assessment of priorities; high tolerance of complexity
(3) *Bases of leaders' authority*	Reward, punishment and legitimate authority	Participative leadership; task-facilitating and representative functions	Complex network of authority based on expertise, commitment and social skills

(4) *Methods for resolving disputes*	Rules, hierarchical authority	Mutual problem-solving, negotiation	Mutual adjustment through open and extensive communications; advocacy combined with review; high tolerance of differences
(5) *Integrating effort*	Individuals are assigned to differentiated tasks and their efforts pooled	Individuals are assigned to the tasks of a group; the efforts of different groups are pooled	Individuals are assigned to workroles that may include special tasks, but normally require competencies which overlap with others; a continuous adjustment of task responsibilities occurs as needs demand and experiences dictate

Tavistock researchers argued that, where possible, instead of dividing jobs into fragmented tasks, autonomous workgroups should be given responsibility for different 'whole tasks', with leaders assuming the role of facilitators and group representatives.

While socio-technical studies consider the relevance of technological factors for organizational structures, other approaches have emphasized the significance of an organization's environment for its internal structuring. As shown in the study by Burns and Stalker (1966), which we mentioned in chapter 3, 'mechanistic' and 'organic' (or 'organismic') structures in organizations show different capacities to adapt to changing circumstances. The former are strongly bureaucratized, relying heavily on hierarchy and rules and on clear lines of demarcation between the task functions of junior level staff and the policy functions of their seniors. Organic organizations, on the other hand, are designed, not for stability, but for changing operating circumstances. Minimal task specifications are provided for their members. A task-and-development orientation is required within them. Task allocation and priorities are continually reviewed, with particular emphasis being placed on relevant knowledge and expertise. A network of authority emerges in an organization that is not based on hierarchical position but on expertise and commitment. Communications are extensive and open within the organization.

In table 5 certain characteristics of bureaucracies, autonomous workgroups and organic structures are compared and important distinctions are illustrated. We would emphasize, however, that the structures described in the figure are only rarely found in a 'pure' form in organizations. In many instances a mixture of types can be seen. Shamir (1978), for example, argues that hotels typically exhibit a mix of mechanistic and organic features, and others have pointed out how management controls, such as budget and production data, often operate against the participative ideal that other aspects of an organization's structure may have been designed to encourage. Indeed, the picture is further complicated by the observation that the extent to which structures influence behaviour patterns in an organization is itself highly variable. In his comments on organization structures in hotels, Shamir argues that, although hotels 'put their staff in uniforms, ask them to perform certain rituals, and limit the scope of their contacts to customers by creating a highly differentiated structure so that each customer is served by several employees and each employee serves many customers' (p. 299), the control this makes possible over customer–employee relations is limited. Hotel staff still show a wide range of attitudes towards their customers. This observation reflects a more general point. While the structure of an organization, as depicted on official documents, may seem precise and ordered, for the members of the organization themselves it sometimes seems undisciplined and chaotic.

While there is some debate as to whether, even in situations in which an organization's task is routine and its environment stable, alternatives to bureaucracies should always be sought, psychologists have argued that there are considerable advantages to developing new approaches to organizational structuring. None the less, in well-established organizations this is not an easy thing to do. The structural characteristics adopted in the early days of an organization's history tend to remain relatively stable over time. As Stinchcombe (1969) argues, this may occur for a number of reasons, for example the original structure may remain the most effective, significant competition may not have emerged to encourage change and vested interests within the organization may have preserved its original form. Be this as it may, some commentators have suggested that the pace of social change in the modern world is outstripping people's capacities to adapt. As we discuss in subsequent chapters, psychologists have developed a range of approaches to help cope with this problem, to help 'unfreeze' organizations and to train people in the social skills that the alternatives to bureaucracies invariably require.

5

Thought and action in organizational psychology

'Many psychologists working today in an applied field are keenly aware of the need for close co-operation between theoretical and applied psychology. This can be accomplished in psychology, as it has been accomplished in physics, if the theorist does not look toward applied problems with highbrow aversion or with a fear of social problems, and if the applied psychologist realises that there is nothing so practical as a good theory. (Lewin, 1967, p. 169)

The scientist/practitioner debate

Organizational psychology, like other fields of applied psychology, poses questions about the relation between theory and practice that are as pertinent today as in 1944 when Lewin first made the observation quoted above from a posthumous collection of his papers. They arise from the different organizational worlds inhabited by those who seek to develop the scientific base of their discipline and those who seek to put their psychological knowledge to use in dealing with practical problems. The former are usually employed in academic institutions and the latter as managers, administrators, researchers or consultants in non-academic organizations of all kinds. While both are interested in 'real-world' issues, such as people's attitudes to their jobs and how these affect their behaviour at work, the ways in which the scientist, on the one hand, and the practitioner, on the other, perceive, define and approach such problems differ radically. These differences are summarized in table 6. They represent contrasting institutionalized systems of value that are expressed in the criteria by which success and failure are judged and the associated behaviour rewarded or penalized. For the scientist, it is important to obtain adequate data that will elucidate the problem in terms of an accepted, conceptual framework and allow generalizations to be made from the results of the study. For the practitioner, what matters is short-term action that will reduce or eliminate the presenting problem, even if its causes and consequences are not fully understood. The scientist looks for approval to the academic community, which evaluates success largely in terms of output of conference papers and publications, whereas the practitioner's success depends on achieving results that are clearly visible to superiors, peers and subordinates as contributing to the overall, organizational goals. To the academic researcher who

Table 6   Comparison of the value and problem-solving assumptions of managers and researchers

	Researchers	Managers
Value assumptions:		
Goal	Understanding	Accomplishment
Criterion of excellence	Validity	Effectiveness
Application	Abstract/ general	Concrete/ specific
Problem-solving assumptions:		
Time perspective	Long-term	Short-term
Methodology	Control inputs for valid explanation	Control inputs for effective influence
Viewpoint	Objective	Involved
A negative result is:	Information	Failure

After Brown (1973).

believes that scientific objectivity requires that the investigator remains detached from the situation studied, it is immaterial whether or not his or her efforts give any practical help to those who have to deal with particular problems. Conversely, to the practitioner it is being able to give this practical assistance that is all-important and it is of little consequence whether or not the investigation contributes to theory or results in scientific publications.

Given these different frames of reference, it is not surprising that there has been much discussion in recent years about the relationship between 'pure' and 'applied' research (Warr, 1978), an associated debate about the roles of scientist and practitioner (Davidson, 1977; de Wolff *et al.*, 1981) and concern among the social science community as a whole as to why organizational research is not more widely used (Beyer and Trice, 1982). Indeed, Cherns (1979) records that:

> I have not been able to trace in practice one example of a study carried out in a university or in a research institute or anywhere else which resulted in direct application except where the researcher has become involved in following through his studies into application. (Cherns, 1979, p. 115)

For this reason, he sees 'action research' as often a more appropriate model for applying psychology in organizations than one based on the natural sciences. In other words, instead of remaining detached and distanced from the problem under investigation, the psychologist becomes actively involved with it. He or she is not there simply to explore, evaluate and report on what he or she observes, with the aim of another publication at the end, but is concerned with applying and implementing the findings in the particular situation studied.

However, although valued and accepted by practitioners, action research has not become the predominant research style favoured by academic organizational psychologists. If anything, it has accentuated the gap between the two communities for a number of reasons. First of all, the action researcher does not choose either the problem or the variables of the study, but agrees these jointly with members of the organization concerned. As a result, the researcher may be required to operate beyond the boundaries of psychology, problems posed by non-psychologists inevitably coming 'problem-shaped' and not packaged under a disciplinary label.

Secondly, there is a political dimension to these negotiations that disturbs some psychologists, as well as related professional and ethical issues which we shall describe later. The move away from deduction and induction, explanation, prediction, detachment and contemplation that action research requires, with its alternative emphasis on conjecture, understanding and engagement, is difficult for those who live and work in an environment embodying traditional, scientific values. Therefore, it is both easier and more comfortable for many academics to concentrate on method-centred, rather than problem-centred, research and so avoid the uncertainties of engagement with the everyday world. In addition, action-research reports may be too confidential for publication, the results of such studies are notoriously difficult to replicate, they may have little direct theoretical relevance and, because of their commitment to their approach, action researchers themselves may be unwilling to admit to the possibility of errors in their work. Thus, to the scientific community, claims to knowledge based on action research are weak in comparison with those based on conventional, experimental methods.

Here again, we must stress that, in looking at different types of applied research, it is the context in which the evaluation is made that is important rather than there being a 'one best way' of developing either theory or practice. We have described the contrasts in order to explain the dissatisfactions of those who think that the social sciences in general, and applied psychology in particular, are failing to deal with the day-to-day difficulties and realities of behaviour in organizations. For example, Susman and Evered (1978), lamenting the remoteness of scholarly journals from the everyday concerns and preoccupations of managers and organizational members, comment that:

> There is a crisis in the field of organizational science. The principal symptom of this crisis is that as our research methods and techniques have become more sophisticated they have also become increasingly less useful for solving the practical problems that numbers of organisations face. (Susman and Evered, 1978, p. 582)

Argyris (1968) has also warned about the unintended consequences of rigorous research, pointing out that the very process by which variables are controlled may themselves produce behaviours that are artefacts of the experimental process.

Nature of applications

To bemoan what is not happening, however, diverts attention from the extent to which psychology has contributed to our understanding of behaviour in organizations, its great potential in helping to solve organizational problems, the ways in which psychological concepts and approaches have permeated thought and action outside the academic community and the multiple roles taken by organizational psychologists in their professional capacities. These positive features are interrelated and their influences are often diffuse, but we shall endeavour to illustrate them with some specific examples. As a framework for this discussion, figure 2 summarizes the relationships between the source of a problem, its definition, resulting action and outcomes from the perspective of psychologists' engagements with organizations. Problems identified by psychologists are usually those arising within the discipline itself, such as the nature of human learning, which may have practical implications. However, it is not the applied aspects that draw attention to the problem initially. The reverse is true of problems identified by outside agencies and referred to psychologists: in this case, it is invariably the social and organizational dimensions that lead to recognition of the problem although this recognition, in turn, may give rise to basic research.

A good example of the way in which fundamental research, prompted by social concern, has contributed significantly to both theory and practice is provided by the history of British psychological research on age and work, reviewed by Welford (1976). In the years of full employment immediately after the Second World War, it was feared that the increasing proportion of older people in the population heralded a serious shortage of labour unless workers were to remain in employment beyond the normal retiring age. Conventional wisdom held that at 50, or even at 40, people were 'too old' for certain jobs and that 'one can't teach an old dog new tricks', so there was much interest in the jobs older people could do and whether they could be taught new skills. The implications for employment in a period when the country was seeking to revive its industry in the aftermath of war predisposed funding bodies to support research on the problem while, at the same time, psychologists became interested in the fundamental changes in human performance that occur with age. Consequently research units concerned with industrial gerontology were

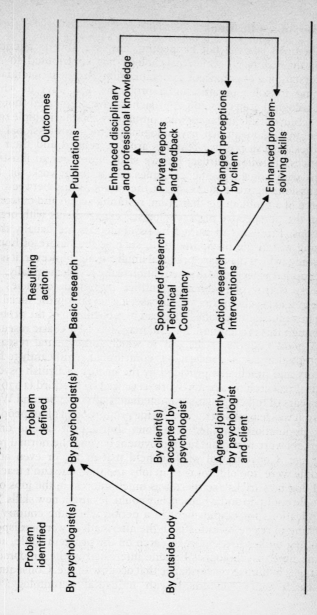

Figure 2 Applying psychology in organizations

established, the first at Cambridge in 1946 and, subsequently, others at Bristol, Liverpool and London, with a number of individual research workers also working on related problems.

In Welford's words, 'the research of the 1940s and 1950s represented a grand endeavour to map out lines of theory in a largely unexplored field' (p. 131). However, he points out that, in comparison with the largely empirical, pre-war American studies of age and work, the Nuffield Unit at Cambridge had the advantage of being able to draw on experimental studies of skill being conducted there which were laying the foundations of information-processing theory. These provided the framework for initial laboratory experiments on ageing, from which questions requiring direct studies in industry were identified. Indeed, the considerable volume of post-war psychological research on ageing comprised a series of reciprocal laboratory-based and empirical investigations, underpinned by theoretical developments in the study of performance in general. These showed that, contrary to what was believed in 1946, the most important changes with age are of central origin, that is they are due to changes in the brain and not to the deterioration of peripheral structures such as muscles, joints or sense organs. As a result, there is a shortening of the immediate memory span and increasing difficulty in recalling material from long-term memory store, factors which account for most of the difficulty shown by older people in learning, especially if taught by methods (lectures, verbal instructions) requiring them to remember what they have been told. However, and equally important from a practical point of view, experiments on methods of training older workers (Belbin, 1964) showed that 'activity learning', in which learners are placed in an active and stimulating situation in which they discover the requisite knowledge for themselves and proceed to make use of it, is beneficial for all age groups, but especially older people.

Other studies reviewed by Welford include examination of the age distributions of people in different jobs (on the assumption that the proportion of older workers in any job is an indication of its suitability for them). These studies have also increased knowledge and changed opinions concerning the capabilities of older people, both in and out of employment. Much of the work on training has diffused into teaching programmes for adults. However, it is ironic that there is unlikely to be any widespread application in the work situation now that unemployment has made older people 'surplus to requirements' in many instances and every effort is being made to persuade them to retire early. In fact, as long ago as 1955, when revised population estimates and the advent of automation indicated that fears about an ageing workforce and acute shortage of labour were groundless, it was realized that it would be undesirable for older people to go on working as long as they wished. Furthermore, it led to a loss of interest in Britain in the whole area of industrial gerontology and the psychological aspects of ageing, none of the research units concerned with these problems surviving for more than a few more years.

This illustrates how the environment in which psychologists work and the climate of opinion relating to applied problems influence the direction of their endeavour, not least because of the attitudes of funding bodies and agencies which give financial support to research. In the case of studies of ageing, this point is reinforced by the different response to the revised population estimates in the USA, where psychological aspects of ageing were defined not in the context of work but of health. The prospect of large numbers of retired people with increased life expectancies was perceived as a matter of social concern and there was a considerable expansion of research in this area. Consequently, as Welford notes, 'the centre of gravity of research on the psychological aspects of ageing shifted from Britain to the USA and has remained there ever since' (Welford, 1976, p. 131).

Another example of the effect of context upon applied research, this time concerning the use of attitude surveys, is given by Williams and Woodward (1983). Attitude surveys have been widely used to assess the views and feelings of members of organizations about their jobs, conditions of employment, managerial style, personnel policy and other organizational aspects likely to be associated with employee morale. Much commissioned research by organizations is in this area. Williams and Woodward describe how, in an attitude survey of all the UK staff working in the British offices of a foreign airline company, the general manager was instrumental not only in commissioning the survey by an external consultant/researcher but also in controlling the uses he was prepared to make of the results. This is contrasted with a survey undertaken in two London hospitals which was planned and executed on a consultative basis, with the results being fed back to the participants and decisions relating to follow-up action being taken at departmental meetings. The credibility of attitude surveys, therefore, depends largely on how the results are utilized so that when, as in the case of the airline, these are treated as confidential to top management, employee morale may deteriorate further if management fails to act in accordance with employees' expressed views and expectations.

Whatever the nature of the problem and the ensuing type of investigation, it is important that the approach taken is congruent with the objectives both of sponsors and clients and of the researchers themselves. As indicated already, timing may be a critical factor here, as is caricatured in the statement that 'the researcher wants to get the right answer, but the manager wants it by Tuesday'! Patrick (1980), commenting on contributions made by psychologists to solving work problems in capital-intensive and continuous process industries, notes that these depend on an adequate job analysis that is often difficult and time-consuming. He points out that the successful use of hierarchical task analysis, combined with a cumulative part method of learning, in developing a training design for a complex planning skill (reported by Shepherd and Duncan, 1980), took about three years. In this instance the time spent was acceptable to management because the problem had been seen as intractable. However, Patrick suggests this may not always be so, either to the organizations concerned or to academic researchers who feel under pressure to publish frequently.

Multiple roles

Psychology therefore offers no instant solutions to complex organizational problems, practitioners and academics alike recognizing the importance of adequate diagnosis and definition of a problem before effective action can be taken. As figure 2 indicates, however, psychologists may have little or no involvement at this stage and the extent and nature of their engagement with an outside organization will depend upon the presenting problem, the type of solution sought and the methods used. These factors, according to Cherns (1976), may result in one of four different roles for the researcher: (i) that of *subordinate technician* to the organization's requirements; (ii) that of *engineer*, able to select only the methods to be used in seeking the types of solution sought by he organization to a specified problem; (iii) that of *consultant*, where only the nature of the problem is specified in advance and he researcher has discretion to deal with it as he or she considers appropriate; (iv) that of *action researcher*, where there is discussion between the parties on all three aspects – nature of the problem, type of solution and methods.

This is a useful categorization, but it is not exhaustive. Other writers have identified other roles: Wallis (1971), for example, considers that the professional activities of psychologists in central government departments and elsewhere include a technical consultancy role, a teaching and training role, an advisory role and an applied research and development role, while Lytle (1975) claims that action research entails the roles of advocate, leader, strategist, expert, conceptualizer, educator, writer, speaker, trainer, training designer, counsellor and process consultant! To this list or, perhaps more accurately, subsuming much of it we would add the role of specialized helper, that is that of assisting others to mobilize their own resources to deal with their own problems. In all kinds of organizational development and change programmes, such as those we discuss in chapter 6, the psychologist is a facilitator, rather than an engineer, who enables people to see and to act differently rather than making them do so.

Viewed in this way, it is apparent that much practice in organizational psychology is supportive and ameliorative in nature, not instrumental. In helping members of organizations to understand and re-define their situations, to plan and execute change, the psychologist acts as a shock-absorber, lubricant or professional buffer – whichever metaphor one prefers – within the system as a whole and protects it, and the individuals who comprise it, from the possible disruptive effects of the strong feelings, fears and anxieties associated with change. By its very nature, this is an inconspicuous role and, perhaps for this reason, apt to be underrated by those who look for clear-cut, tangible results.

It should be noted, however, that these various roles are not necessarily restricted to psychologists. We use the word 'psychologist' here for convenience, but, as mentioned earlier, the boundaries of organizational psychology overlap with those of other disciplines. Consequently, much organizational research and application is multi-disciplinary and undertaken by other social scientists as well as psychologists. Furthermore, there has been a diffusion of social science ideas among practitioners, writers on management and management trainers that has led to concepts and techniques developed by psychologists being used by those with no formal training in the subject.

'Giving psychology away'

The incorporation of social science perspectives in management education and the influence of psychological theories on the thought and outlook of consultants and teachers accords with Miller's (1969) plea, in his presidential address to the American Psychological Association, to 'give psychology away'. He argued that psychological knowledge should be passed freely to all who need and can use it in the interests of promoting human welfare, rather than be confined to members of the profession.

In the realm of organizational psychology, a fair amount has been given away already, as indicated above. To take but one example, concepts of motivation associated with the work of American social scientists such as Maslow (1954), Argyris (1957, 1964) and Herzberg (1966) are now widely known and espoused in principle, even if they do not always form the basis of managerial action. These writers have been prominent in drawing attention to the unrealized human potential apparent in many systems of work organization. In their view, people are capable of considerable achievement and self-realization when given the appropriate environment, but are liable to become awkward and unresponsive when placed in a situation requiring only a fraction of their potential. Uncooperative behaviour and lack of motivation on the part of employees are attributable, therefore, to systems of work organization and managerial control based on assumptions, called by McGregor (1960) Theory X, that people are inherently lazy and have to be induced by external goads and incentives to work to the standards of performance expected by the organization.

What Schein (1980) calls the self-actualization assumptions, termed by McGregor Theory Y, underpin the advocacy of managerial strategies that will make work intrinsically more meaningful and challenging to people who will, it is claimed, thereby commit themselves to directing their energies toward organizational objectives. Maslow's concept of a hierarchy of human needs is frequently cited in support of this approach, that is the desirability of re-organizing routine tasks so as not to frustrate the individual's higher needs. He postulates that it is only unsatisfied needs which motivate behaviour and that only when a person's basic physical and safety needs are regularly and adequately met do social, ego and self-esteem needs come to the fore. At the apex of this hierarchy are the self-actualization needs, that is the need to make full use of all one's talents and resources.

Although this is a difficult theory to test empirically and evidence for the hierarchical ordering of motives is weak, it has an inherent appeal and face validity in explaining why different needs and motives may be expected to operate in different situations (e.g. a starving man will seek bread rather than education). For this reason and because it has often been presented as a prescription for 'good' management practice (i.e. design your organization and managerial strategies to encourage self-actualization and people will voluntarily integrate their own goals with those of the organization), it permeates much of the advice offered to managers and others concerning motivation at work. Indeed, 'self-actualization' is becoming a term in common parlance.

Valuable as this formulation has been in challenging outmoded views of behaviour and alerting a wider public to the issues involved, it has drawbacks if offered as a simplistic prescription for universal application. For example, it discounts the possibility that some people may wish for less, rather than more, involvement in their work in order that they may realize their potentialities more effectively off the job. Likewise it fails to recognize that, as a person is a 'twenty-four hour animal', there are limits to the self-development that can be achieved in any one setting. It also implies the possibility of overcoming technological constraints in the design of work that may not be amenable to change or modification.

In giving psychology away, therefore, it is important that useful ideas and tentative theories are seen for what they are and not presented as overgeneralized statements that ignore social, cultural and individual differences. Psychology has no universal panaceas for organizational problems, but, in conjunction with other social sciences, it can provide an appreciation of the multiple dimensions of behaviour in organizations. What is offered is an insightful, analytical approach that will help people to identify for themselves the sources of their problems and assist them to discover their own solutions.

Professional issues

The examples cited above highlight the fact that action in organizational psychology is directed primarily towards problem-solving, expecially on behalf of those who govern and manage. However, whereas before the mid- to late 1960s this was an unproblematic issue for applied psychologists, most of whom believed implicitly that their contributions were both useful and beneficial to society, they are now sensitive to the possibility of appearing to be 'lackeys of management' and aware that, in engagements with organizations, it is easy to become a pawn in another's game. For those whose personal values and/or ideological commitment lead them to identify with those whom they see as disadvantaged members of society, it may be difficult to reconcile their desire to assist the latter with the knowledge that access to them is dependent on those whose interests they may not wish to further. For instance, feminists are unlikely to be able to undertake research on women at work without the assent of male bosses and trade union officials.

Concern about who are the beneficiaries of organizational psychologists' activities, and for whose benefit they could and should be looking, is symptomatic of the current social and intellectual climate in which many formerly unquestioned assumptions are being challenged, such as the notion that science is value-free. Within psychology generally a fundamental issue has been the extent to which the scientific study of human behaviour assumes deterministic explanations and the extent to which the results of such study can be used to manipulate and control. In organizational psychology, where a strong interest is shown in the conditions under which people co-operate effectively together, the responsibility for added vigilance concerning the possible uses of the subject seems clear. For, whether they like it or not, psychologists employed in and by organizations have to engage with the prevailing system if they are to operate at all. Often the initial task through which they establish their credibility, for example, designing a selection procedure, entails their taking a technocratic role or implying support for the orientations and values of the sponsoring organization, as in the case of action research. How far they are able to shape the situation to accord with their own values and how far they accommodate to the norms of those with whom they work will vary with each individual and each engagement. Whatever guidance they may receive from their

Table 7 Steps designed to mitigate the manipulative aspects of behaviour change in each of three social science roles

Desirable steps	Role of practitioner	Role of applied researcher	Role of basic researcher
(1) Increasing awareness of manipulation	Labelling own values to self and clients; allowing client to 'talk back'	Evaluating organization that will use findings; considering by whom, how, and in what context they will be used	Predicting probabilities of different uses of research product, given existing socio-historical context
(2) Building protection against or resistance to manipulation into the process	Minimizing own values and maximizing client's values as dominant criteria for change	Helping target group to protect its interests and resist encroachments on its freedom	Studying processes of resistance to control, and communicating findings to the public
(3) Setting enhancement of freedom of choice as a positive goal	Using professional skills and relationship to increase client's range of choices and ability to choose	Promoting opportunities for increased choice on part of target group as integral features of the planned change	Studying conditions for enhancement of freedom of choice and maximization of individual values

Kelman (1965).

fellow professionals, ultimately it rests with the individual psychologist or social scientist to define his or her standards of professional conduct.

This is not an easy matter in a field in which the well-intentioned efforts of some to introduce changes that, in their view, will lead to an improved quality of working life may be construed by others as forms of manipulation and control. For example, van Strien (1978) suggests that 'having a weak spot for democracy' many psychologists put a lot of effort into participation programmes and the humanization of work which, in reality, serve to create a barrier against any fundamental redistribution of power in the organization, although the psychologists do not perceive this. He continues: 'It is often their misfortune to meet distrust and obstruction from the workers who often view consultation and job design programmes as tricks on the part of management to squeeze more from them, or to make some jobs redundant' (van Strien, 1978, p.298). In his opinion, the appropriate stance for psychologists associated with such programmes is to make clear to the workers that the aim of the project is to make better use of the organization's human resources and let them decide whether to enter the game.

Kelman (1965) argues that the process of influencing or manipulating others is an 'ethically ambiguous act' that violates a fundamental value, but that it is impossible to avoid some degree of control or manipulation when intervening in or seeking to influence human affairs. He therefore proposes some practical steps that psychologists might take to minimize these manipulative aspects which are reproduced in table 7. The practitioner, applied researcher and basic researcher should, according to these suggestions, be alert to the possibilities of manipulation, and aware of defences against it that might enhance freedom of choice as a positive goal.

Although these recommendations are somewhat simplistic in that they take no account of the competing and conflicting interests and power struggles within organizations, which may place psychologists between opposing groups and factions all hoping to gain advantage over the others, they help to clarify the issues involved. Organizational psychologists do face dilemmas concerning their professional responsibilities, but these are no greater than those faced by anyone who has to intervene in the affairs of everyday life.

6

Approaches to organizational change

> We trained hard, but it seemed that every
> time we were beginning to form up into
> teams we would be re-organized. I was to
> learn late in life that we tend to meet any
> new situation by re-organizing, and a
> wonderful method it can be for creating
> the illusion of progress while producing
> confusion, inefficiency and
> demoralisation. (Gaius Petronius, AD 66)

Understanding change

Given the pervasiveness of organizations in today's world it is clear
that the topic of organizational change is of considerable importance. Attempts to make organizations more efficient, democratic,
responsive or convivial can, if successful, lead to lasting personal
and social benefits. If unsuccessful, however, the frustration and
resentment people experience may themselves compound any
previous problems. Psychologists have contributed a great deal
both to the understanding of reactions to change and to the
development of techniques for its effective management. In
this chapter we review the relevance of certain social psychological concepts to the topic before reviewing a number of the

techniques of organizational development that psychology has pioneered.

It is fair to note that, despite the importance of the topic, popular understanding of organizational change remains at a low level. Two common stereotypes can be identified in the popular culture of our times and in the conventional wisdom served to managers. The first is an optimistic approach. Government agencies are helpful and responsive in the radio soap opera *The Archers*, prisons are jolly places in the TV series *Porridge*, authoritarian and domineering supervisors are harmless enough in *Are You Being Served?* The reassuring images of organizations offered in such productions suggests that, in general, what happens in organizations is all for the best and that suggestions for improvement will be well received. In stark contrast, however, are the dismal visions of organization portrayed in Kafka's novels, or in films like *Bonnie and Clyde* or *One Flew Over the Cuckoo's Nest*. In these, organizations are shown as repressing and unresponsive, to be avoided or to be destroyed.

Such popular stereotypes have their counterparts in much of the literature on change that is available to managers. Mangham (1980), for example, has pointed to the reassuring and blandly optimistic tone of many writers on 'organizational development', quoting as typical the promise of one that 'radical change is possible and that any reasonably intelligent and able manager *can* attain it in his organization' (Mangham, p. 361). Others, such as Watson (1976), suggest that resistance to change is both blind and seemingly inevitable. In reality, the responses people show to change are many and varied. To begin to understand this variation it is necessary to avoid simplistic approaches and examine reactions to change at the individual, group and organizational levels.

At the *individual* level, one approach is to study in detail how people respond to significant disruptions in their lives. This method was adopted by Marris (1974), who developed a general model of reaction to change from his analysis of the experience of bereavement. The sudden loss of a loved one is a terrible experience which can fundamentally upset the life of the bereaved. Initially, the death leaves a bereaved person shocked and distraught, physically distressed, vulnerable to poor health. The loss is too great fully to be comprehended in the early phases. Grieving individuals find they are both unable and unwilling to surrender their past and the loved one who was a central part of it. So they brood, cling to the possessions of the dead beloved, even sensing his or her presence around them. The acute phase of grief will last for several weeks. Later phases are typified by feelings of apathy and hostility directed both at self and at others. The experience of grief abates only slowly, perhaps taking a year or more, and may be prolonged extensively if expressions of pain and mourning are unnaturally suppressed.

The essence of Marris' contribution to understanding reactions to changes is his analysis of grieving itself. The bereaved, he points out, show a number of ambivalent responses. They may complain of loneliness, yet shun the company of others; though complaining if others avoid them, they may rebuff sympathizers; while saying there is nothing to live for, they may hurry back to work, and so on. Marris interprets 'inconsistencies' of this kind as expressions of a conflict between two contradictory impulses. First, the bereaved person wishes to return to the time before the death which, as this is impossible, leads to consolidation of what remains of value from the relationship to prevent further loss. There is a deep desire to remain faithful to the memory and past significance of the one who has been lost. Second, the bereaved individual begins to reach forward to a situation where the past can be forgotten. A new life must be built without the other. It is, Marris argues, through grief and mourning that these contradictory impulses become resolved so that loss of the person is accepted without the loss of what he or she meant. Thus the numbness and despair of early grief and the later attempts to build a new life gradually meld together and a re-integration is achieved, when the past is neither abandoned nor embraced but its memory informs the present with valid meanings.

The death of a loved one is, of course, a traumatic experience; the loss is total, normally sudden and shocking, and touches people at the deepest levels. But Marris' analysis of grieving and re-integration is relevant to other changes, particularly his stress on the importance of subjective meanings in understanding re-actions to change. He shows that some consistency in people's key purposes and attachments is crucial for their well-being and that, paradoxical as it may seem, without such a basic consistency, people's abilities to cope with changing environments and to develop significant new directions are impaired. To protect key meanings we will defend the contexts within which they developed. Reason, persuasion and argument by others are not enough to help people adjust to significant losses, for no-one can solve for someone else the crisis of re-integration that disruptive changes impose. Changes which appear reasonable and straightforward to some may, in altogether unforeseen ways, undermine certain key attachments that are felt by others.

In similar vein, *at the group level of analysis*, a great deal can be learned about social norms from the defences against unwelcome changes which are mounted by group representatives. As we noted in chapter 4, groups serve many functions in people's lives and their behaviour is influenced by the norms of the groups to which they belong. Group norms, which may operate unobtrusively in normal circumstances, often appear in sharp relief when changes pose a threat to the group. Therefore, rather than trying to overcome resistance to change by outmanoeuvering any opposition from within the group, it is better to regard this as behaviour directed towards group preservation. Tactics such as procrastination, objection to the logic of the proposed change, arguments that the time is not right or that significant others will not be happy with the proposals will then be recognized as distress symptoms that merit further enquiry.

The concept of 'role', that we discussed in earlier chapters, is particularly useful when analysing how groups respond to change. While the term can be used to refer simply to the expectations groups have of their members, its origins in the language of stage and theatre are of particular relevance here. Foremost among theorists using the term in this fashion is Goffman (1959), who maintains that a person's behaviour in the presence of others is analogous to the performance of a theatrical actor. People therefore seek to control the impressions they convey to others by the way they play their social roles and, in so doing, to influence situations to their own ends. This is not to say that Goffman is referring only to occasions when people pretend to be something other than they are. His analogy suggests that social life consists of communications and the management of messages by active beings seeking to realize their purposes in their exchanges with others. Roles, setting, appearance, and manner are used expressively ('dramaturgically') to establish contact and to fashion social interactions. How effectively we play our parts depends on our social skills and how perceptive we are of the impressions others are seeking to create. The analogy with the theatre only breaks down when it is realized that, in real life, people often play their roles largely unaware that they are doing so. Whereas, on the stage, actors interpret, rehearse and later perform their roles within specific bounds of space and time, in everyday life people interpret, rehearse and perform simultaneously, improvising and adjusting as the situation demands in a manner more akin to *avant garde* than classical theatre.

Mangham (1978) uses the dramaturgical analogy to analyse change within organizations, maintaining that the process by which social actors perceive, interpret and respond to the impressions given by others is of the same order whether the social interaction be between two people, within a small group or a larger, more formal body:

> The processes of interpretation and performance which constitute action in ICI boardrooms and in cabinet offices are not unique; there is nothing specifically 'organizational' about them which distinguishes them from processes occurring between courting couples, knockabout comedians, members of a family or participants in a charabanc outing. (Mangham, 1978, p. 57)

What distinguishes these 'organizational' encounters are the settings or situations in which they occur. These may shape the form and style of the performance, but the latter itself, Mangham argues, 'still unfolds with a regularity and similarity of process which transcends the particular setting'. It is the product of the 'situational script', the relatively predetermined behaviours expected in particular circumstances (behaviour in a library, for example, follows a different script from that appropriate to a cafe or a bar) and the opportunity this affords people to indulge their 'personal scripts', that is performances which lead to a satisfying portrayal of the images they wish to present of themselves.

Following this analogy with the theatre, it is apparent that it is only certain participants in the drama, and at certain times, whose attempts to re-fashion the guiding scripts are likely to be well received. The situational scripts operating in a group are the outcome of successive social interactions. At least some of the key actors will find them satisfactory – many may feel they 'own' them – while others may have been recruited into the group because of their willingness to adopt certain roles. Consequently, attempts to 'tear up' a situational script and impose another are unlikely to be acceptable; change may occur, but is likely to take place slowly, not least because of the influence of personal scripts. Suggestions that their performances are inadequate or that the demands of the role are changing and that they too need to change can be particularly hard for people to take. Much will also depend on who suggests the proposed change and the manner of its presentation: if this is perceived as patronizing or arrogant the other social actors may well bring into play their repertoire of resisting or 'putting-down the other person' behaviour.

At the *organizational* level of analysis, linked to both concepts of situational scripts and of dominant ideologies, is the concept of organizational culture. Harrison (1972) identified four typical cultures in organizations according to their underlying value systems. These are designated role, task, power and person cultures. An organization that is *role oriented* relies on agreements, rules and regulations. Emphasis is placed on appropriate procedures, on rights and duties, on status and hierarchy. Organizations that are closely regulated by law, such as banks and insurance companies, are likely examples of role-oriented cultures. A *task-oriented* organization, on the other hand, places far less emphasis on order and predictability. Here the accent is upon the achievement of a particular goal to which members are committed. Small organizations are more likely to show this orientation than large ones, entrepreneurial businesses or research teams being good examples. *Power-oriented* organizations show a competitive, jealous, domineering and exploitative attitude in their external relations, while internally, competition between executives can be keen and sometimes ruthless. Certain large international organizations fall into this class. Finally, *person-oriented* organizations are those which develop solely to meet the needs of their constituent members. Their structure is minimal as personal growth, conviviality or excitement may be more important than any superordinate objective. Rural craft co-operatives and communes provide examples here. Harrison suggests that these four cultures will respond in distinctive ways to pressures for change. This is illustrated in table 8.

Another perspective on organizational change, at a more general level of abstraction, is provided by open systems theory. This, as we discussed in chapter 1, emphasizes the inter-dependencies of the constituent parts of an organization and the homeostatic

	Individual members' opportunities to pursue growth and development needs independent of organizational goals	Organization's effectiveness in responding to dangerous or threatening environments	Organization's ability to deal rapidly and effectively with environmental complexity and change
Within a role culture:	Low: (Organization goals are relatively rigid and activities closely proscribed)	Moderate to low: (The organization is slow to mobilize to meet increases in threat)	Low: (Slow to change normal routines; communication channels are easily over-loaded)
Within a task culture:	Low: (The individual should not be in the organization if s/he does not subscribe to some of its goals)	Moderate to high: (The organization may be slow to make decisions but produces highly competent responses)	High: (Flexible assignment of resources and short communication channels facilitate adaptation)
Within a power culture:	Low: (Unless one is in a sufficiently high position to determine organization goals)	High: (The organization tends to be perpetually ready for a fight)	Moderate to low: (Depends on size; pyramidal communication channels are easily overloaded)
Within a person culture:	High: (Organization goals are determined by individual need)	Low: (The organization is slow to become aware of threat and slow to mobilize effort against it)	High: (But response is erratic; assignment of resources to problem depends greatly on individual needs and interests)

After Harrison (1972).

relationship between the organization and its environment, so that a change in any one element results in changes in the others in order to restore equilibrium. For example, a change in technology will lead to new training needs, new pay procedures, promotion opportunities and so on, with accompanying shifts in the balance of power within and between groups. Such ramifications are not always easy to anticipate, that is many changes planned for reasons of technical efficiency have floundered because of their likely implications for other aspects of an organization.

Likewise, in a multiplicity of ways, the environment of an organization affects its internal operations. This environment includes the demand for the organization's products and services, the legislative framework within which it must operate, the social values of the community from which it draws its members and the extent to which such factors are stable or changing. Misreading of their environments can imperil organizations' powers of survival and writers on organizations from different traditions now acknowledge the influence of environmental factors on internal organizational structures and functions. Therefore, if any significant internal changes in an organization are to be sustained, it will need to relate to its environment in new ways.

Introducing change: a case study

The 1960s were characterized by optimism on the part of social scientists about 'planned organizational change' and a corresponding interest by large organizations in what the social sciences had to offer them. In Shell UK a number of factors led the top management team to review the total operations of the company and to seek new approaches to managing their workforce. Among these factors were the Suez crisis, the advent of OPEC, demarcation disputes in oil refining, increasing signs of unhappiness with the then paternalistic style of the company and the fact that its major competitor had introduced new working arrangements. A special project team suggested that many of the company's organizational problems were the fault, not of the employees, but of the way the employees had been treated. It was decided, therefore, that managers should adopt a new series of assumptions about human nature and develop new managerial practices based upon these psychological insights. Accordingly, consultants from the

Tavistock Institute of Human Relations were asked to write a new philosophy of management for Shell, based on socio-technical systems theory and the concept of 'joint optimization' of the psychological and technical demands of jobs. This philosophy was then debated throughout the company in conferences specially organized for this purpose, first by the top management team, then by groups of middle managers and lastly by plant operators and maintenance men over a period of two years. It was hoped that when sufficient people were convinced of the value of the new approach a shift would occur in the climate of the company.

It should be emphasized, at this point, that the change attempt at Shell was undertaken at a time when very little was known about changes in complex organizations. As a result, it incorporated some of the common misconceptions about managing change that we described at the beginning of the chapter. Three features, in particular, should be noted: it was a change conceived and introduced from the top down; the focus of the change effort was on individuals and their values; the architects of the change programme set out to achieve widespread change *en bloc*.

What happened is summarized in figure 3 which compares early reports of apparent success with the findings of a later study showing that the programme failed to produce lasting change. The bottom of the first vertical column shows four main avenues of dissemination that emerged from the philosophy conferences: demonstration of job re-design projects, managers acting more participatively, new contractual relationships with blue-collar staff (salaried staff status was exchanged for the abolition of certain restrictive practices) and the design and building of a new refinery, based on the principles of the new philosophy. In the event, none of these developments was very successful and, as the final column shows, the lasting legacy of the Shell philosophy was less one of gratitude by staff that new, more acceptable, approaches to organization had been introduced and more one of disappointment and cynicism that fine promises had failed to materialize.

To understand these outcomes, we must return to the main features of the change programme that we noted earlier. First, the exercise was introduced from the top downwards. It was senior management who felt the need for a new approach, but it was middle management who would principally have to adopt new behaviours. The senior managers also assumed that the philosophy would be welcomed by junior level staff, because it stressed

Figure 3 The course of Shell's new philosophy-of-management programme. (After Blackler and Brown, 1980a)

| The top management approve the philosophy | Document accepted as valid and appropriate. Top managers each undertook to manage in accord with its principles. Varied enthusiasm, some reservations expressed but overall strong support reported | The top management at one refinery were mostly enthusiastic. Those at the other main refinery were less so. 'We had to do something as the top man wanted to go this way' |
| Debating the philosophy within the organization | Conferences regarded as generally successful in imparting an understanding of the philosophy and its management implications. A minority of staff enthusiastic, a minority unconvinced. Overall verdict that the conferences were very successful | Many staff did not really understand the philosophy. But there was a momentum of hope and optimism: 'This *was* good stuff, this *was* right, this *was* the long-term thing to do'. Interesting discussions but some resentment at alleged 'brainwashing' |

As originally reported in Hill (1971)

Findings of retrospective study

Demonstration job re-design	Mixed outcomes with some disappointments. Overall, demonstrated the potential value of job re-design to the refineries	The projects raised high expectations that they later dashed. Did not inspire confidence; not imitated as was intended
Managers as change agents	Some examples of successfully self-directed efforts, e.g. an 'experiment' at a wax-generating plant. Briefing sessions were held to help managers run departmental philosophy discussions and to do socio-technical analysis	Managers concerned found pressures on them to innovate became less pressing and less credible. A major 'success' of the philosophy, the wax plant, was to become regarded as a disaster
Introducing the productivity deals	The philosophy was judged to have been of significant help in introducing the deals, the manner of their introduction (joint working parties) being a major innovation. Prospects believed good for continuing success	The joint working parties were aided by the philosophy but increasingly were characterized less by collaboration and more by management manoeuvres. Later, the deals greatly disappointed workers
Designing a new refinery	The principles of job design contained in the philosophy were used at design stage. Innovatory terms and conditions of work. Some difficulties later developed	The Teesport refinery was influenced by the philosophy, but little unusual resulted. Early problems with job designs

their involvement and participation. But, as we saw from our discussion of grief and mourning, change introduced without attention to the felt needs of those most affected is likely to run into difficulties. Efforts were certainly made at the philosophy conferences to debate the pros and cons of the new approach, but its evident support by top management, the lavish settings in which the conferences were held, and the presence of prestigious outside consultants all combined to induce people to accept the philosophy. Disagreements were apt to be seen as 'problems' that people were having with the philosophy, not as statements of legitimate, alternative views. While some people were impressed, others felt they had little choice and yet others felt resentful that the philosophy was being foisted upon them. Many junior level employees certainly were suspicious about management's intentions. Therefore, the philosophy never came to be 'owned' by a substantial number of people throughout the company, but remained the brainchild of top management.

The problems of an exclusively 'top down' approach were compounded by the second feature of the change strategy, namely, that it focused on individuals and their values. As we noted earlier, the roles people play, the norms they observe and many of their values are the result of their experiences in groups. If groups, rather than individuals, are made the focus of change, people have the support of other group members in their individual resolves and attempts to change their behaviour. The Shell philosophy conferences were attended by aggregates of those of similar rank from a number of sites, rather than being comprised of work groups who knew each other well. Furthermore, the meetings were essentially occasions for discussion and were not structured to give participants practice in developing the social skills they might need to implement the new philosophy.

Finally, the aim was to change the culture of the company, fundamentally and speedily. Believing that past practices in Shell had been based on outmoded assumptions, it was thought that the implications of the new philosophy would have far-reaching effects. At a rational level, this analysis was correct, but, even if substantial numbers of staff had been convinced of the value of the new philosophy and been able to develop the skills and roles to manage in accordance with it, they could not have changed the whole organization 'at a stroke'. The implications for organization structure, leadership style, decision-making processes, distribution of power within the company and for Shell's relations with outside organizations were underestimated, as were the inter-active effects of changes in any one of these elements on the rest.

Change strategies

The failure of the Shell project raises the question of the options that are available in attempting to introduce changes in an organization. A useful overview is given by Chin and Benne (1969) who identify the historical roots of different approaches. They distinguish three broad types. First, *rational–empirical* approaches to change are those which emphasize the power of reason and the significance of data and evidence. An example of such a strategy would be efforts to change people through education or reasoned argument, by conducting operational research or organizational analysis and feeding back the results for administrators to apply. *Power–coercive* approaches, on the other hand, are based on creating pressure to compel others to change their practices. Examples include political and legal measures, protest movements (either violent or non-violent) and other pressure groups. Third, Chin and Benne distinguish *normative–re-educative* approaches of the kind employed by therapists, trainers and organizational psychologists. Counselling, group dynamics and psychoanalysis come into this category, together with other approaches that stress the importance of psychological factors. Many of these methods were developed because of the ineffec-tiveness of the alternative strategies. Research reports, for exam-ple, are often filed away and forgotten and intimations of force often lead to resentment, subterfuge and opposition. Normative–re-educative approaches, however, seek to help people to 'own' both their problems and the solutions they find for themselves.

Foremost among organizational psychologists working in the normative–re-educative mode is Chris Argyris, whose theory of action we discussed in chapter 4. In his view, the achievement of change should not be the criterion by which a consultant's work is judged nor should consultants work in organizations with particu-lar changes as their goal. Instead, the main aim of interventionists should be to create the conditions under which their clients may begin to engage actively with their own difficulties and to help new 'self-directing' organizational systems emerge. This will entail, according to Argyris (1970), first, helping people to generate *valid information*; second, creating the conditions under which *free and* *informed choices* can be made around such data; and third, creating conditions under which people will feel *internal commitment* to the decisions reached. Valid information, in this context, includes information about feelings and interpersonal behaviour as an important element, information that is usually suppressed or overlooked in formal, hierarchically structured organizations.

Sensitivity training (or 'T' group training) seemed to offer a way in which psychologists could help people learn about such matters. A 'T' (training) group consists of a small group of people (often previously unknown to one another) who meet to discuss and review the interpersonal dynamics that take place between them. No formal agenda is brought to the meeting or developed within it and there is no conventional task to achieve. Therefore the ways in which members cope with the very unstructured nature of the group are used in the exploration of personal styles. 'T' group trainers have no fixed objectives for their groups, but either by acting as exemplars for other group members (i.e acting in an open and direct way to explore the 'here-and-now' behaviour of the group) or as group-process consultants (i.e occasionally offering interpretations of what is happening in the group), they try to help members to learn from the experience. Typically, such a group will develop through various stages, with early reserved discussion gradually giving way to more frank and open exchanges. Through such a process people can become more aware of their defences and stereotypes and of the benefits of more open and trusting behaviours.

'T' groups enjoyed a great vogue in the 1960s and were championed by many as part of a significant movement that would bring about humanistic reforms in work organizations. In retrospect, the enthusiasm associated with such approaches to interpersonal skills-training now seems very much a part of the general optimism of that era, when, in the industrialized west, greater personal freedom and self-expression was much in evidence. Nowadays, there is far less confidence that concentration on interpersonal styles alone will solve fundamental organizational problems, or that groups can necessarily solve their own problems simply by exploring their own interpersonal processes. The emphasis in the 'T' group of process before task, feelings rather than cognitions, informal rather than formal relations and individuals' needs rather than organizational demands came to be severely criticized. For example, Dunnette and Campbell (Dunnette *et al.* 1968) debated with Argyris whether 'T' group training was as successful in developing task effective groups as it was for people's personal development. Others questioned whether the values of openness and trust can be accepted in organizations which function on different principles. As people realized that the organizational context in which a group works and factors such as the structure of its task and the mix of its members are, in addition to interpersonal skills, of considerable importance in explaining the norms it will display, there was a shift away from using 'T' groups and the like as major change strategies.

However, a number of lessons from this period continue to be valid. The emphasis that Argyris placed on helping people solve their own problems remains as important as it ever was, although now a broader range of primary tasks for organizational interventionists would be articulated than the three he proposed. Emphasis on the group as the focus for change continues to have validity, but the 'valid information' which consultants can help their clients consider will be broader than group-process data alone. It is not now generally believed that unstructured 'T' group methods are particularly successful in developing task effectiveness (see, for example, Levine and Cooper 1976).

The basic approach of interventionist activities to bring about organizational change remains in the normative–re-educative tradition, although the techniques used tend to be both more pragmatic and more eclectic than previously. Three developments should be noted: intervention techniques tend to be more task related, to include structural factors, and related training experiences are less open ended and more focused. These advances in technique have developed alongside changing expectations: hopes that widespread changes will follow the introduction of social science ideas have been replaced by more limited, pragmatic and incremental objectives. In table 9 a typology of 'organizational development' (OD) techniques is presented, ordered according to their relative 'depth' in tackling issues related to change. Thus, operations-analysis techniques, techniques for influencing work performances and techniques for exploring the style in which people work are distinguished from interventions which bring personal values into direct focus. These last interventions, according to Harrison (1970), are to be used only when

97

Table 9 Examples of organizational development interventions

Focus of intervention	Example	Description
Analysing operations	Survey feedback	Members of an organization or department express their attitudes (usually anonymously by questionnaire) about their jobs and organization. The information is used as the basis for general discussion and review
	Role analysis	Job holders examine the expectations significant others (e.g. their bosses, subordinates, work colleagues) have of them in their roles. By comparing these to their own priorities and the expectations of key 'role senders' conflicts and ambiguities can be resolved
Employee performances	Performance counselling	The priorities of a job are reviewed by the employee and his/her immediate supervisor. The adequacy of backup resources are also considered. Specific objectives are agreed and at a suitable future date are reviewed in a further joint planning session
	Job re-design	The design of jobs is examined to explore the extent to which they meet psychological criteria (see discussion in chapter 7). This process, and the re-design of jobs it may lead to, is conducted in a participative way.
Interpersonal relations	Team-process review	Time is made available for the members of a working group

Focus of Intervention	Example	Description
		to discuss its performance and modes of operation. The objective is to bring difficulties into the open so that group members can collaborate in the development of more effective strategies
	Intergroup interventions	Members of two interdependent groups meet to review the expectations they each have of the other and the stereotype views that may have developed. Real and imagined differences are distinguished and, normally with the help of a 'third party' appropriate action is planned
Personal styles and values	Life planning	Individuals work on a series of tasks designed to help them reflect on their past, present and futures. They are encouraged to distinguish between their 'superficial' and 'overriding' purposes (i.e. necessary trivia and crises) and their 'sustaining' purposes in life
	Sensitivity training	An unstructured group meeting when, with the help of an experienced trainer, participants have the opportunity to examine the impact of their interpersonal styles and to explore the efficacy of new social skills and attitudes

they are essential to clients in developing lasting solutions to their problems.

Organizational development

'Organizational development' has replaced 'planned organizational change' as the preferred term of consultants and practitioners who work in this area, perhaps because development implies growth and maturing, whereas planned change might be no more than a deliberate transition from one unsatisfactory state to another. Be this as it may, OD covers a broad range of change strategies designed to enhance both people and organizations in the way they operate. As practised, OD takes many forms, different practitioners having their own preferred orientations. None the less, certain common themes can be identified in this diversity. The difficulties of changing organizations and the need to analyse change processes at the various levels discussed earlier in this chapter are now quite widely recognized. It is also more generally appreciated that much OD work has a political dimension to it. Openness and authenticity as goals are political demands that run contrary to the prevailing personal and situational scripts found in many work organizations. The processes of helping individuals and groups to become more self-determining will, if they are successful, lead to changes in the patterns of influence within their organizations, challenging traditional prerogatives of both managements and trade unions alike. It means too that consultants are rarely confident that they can sensibly regard the total organization as their client. Hopeful as they may be that the benefits of their work will generalize throughout the organization, organizational psychologists are now far more likely to regard their clients as the particular individuals, groups or coalitions with whom they work on a consultancy assignment. They may, indeed, come to identify with these sub-groups rather than with the senior executives who sought their aid initially. In other instances, consultants may feel obliged to withdraw from the situation because their values and those of the client group are too divergent. Change agents, therefore, need to decide in whose interests they are happy to work and, perhaps, how partial they are prepared to let the results of their work become.

In this, psychological consulting within organizations often has a more tactical feel about it than used to be the case. There are four key tasks an organizational change agent is likely to pursue nowadays: *first*, to work with the felt needs of the client group; *second*, to help people mobilize themselves to take action based on these needs; *third*, to help them to set realistic goals; and *fourth*, to help them achieve these within their organizations. These key areas of activity are shown in table 10, which illustrates the important features likely to be associated with success or failure in planned organization change programmes within each key area.

The consultant is likely to be working on some or all of the key tasks simultaneously, rather than in sequence. Moreover, their interdependence means that development is most likely to occur in both the client's capacity to tackle problems and in the problems he or she is prepared to tackle. For example, through working with the client's 'felt needs' it may become apparent to the client that the 'presenting problem' is a symptom of other issues. The areas listed in table 10, therefore, should not be regarded as discrete, but as interlocking and interdependent aspects of a tactical approach to change management.

Table 10 Key tasks in planned organization change and possible characteristics of success

Key issues	Possible characteristics of unsuccessful and successful change attempts		
(1) *Interest groups and felt needs* – who owns the changes?	Antipathy or opposition felt by those affected by the proposals	v.	'Felt needs' served for those involved in the programme
	Support from authoritative groups absent	v.	Support (though not domination) of respected groups
	By-passing existing authority structures	v.	Using existing authority structures
	Many 'gatekeepers' to be satisfied	v.	Few approval channels to be satisfied
(2) *Intervention strategies* – how might people be helped to mobilize their energies?	Authoritarian direction or project seen to belong to enthusiasts only	v.	Widespread participation/control of programme by those affected by it
	Primary advocates of the change distant or unaccepted	v.	Primary advocates accepted as insiders
	Critical assessments of project disapproved of	v.	Open assessments encouraged
	Prepackaged solution introduced	v.	Selection of 'custom-built' solutions developed

(3) *Objectives* – how can these be made realistic?	Objectives unlimited or general	v. Aims limited
	Programme goals unmodified	v. Evolving programme goals
	Aims indeterminate	v. Objectives clear
	Objectives poorly communicated	v. Informed awareness of aims widespread
(4) *Integration issues* – how can the changes be effected within the organization?	Changes pursued regardless of problems for existing norms, values or structures	v. Risks of incompatibility minimized by incremental or pilot introduction permitting possible reversal to old methods
	Inadequate rewards for involvement	v. Adequate rewards associated with involvement
	Lack of competent staff/training or resource support	v. Sufficient resources backup
	Success of new methods for other areas unclear	v. Relative advantages of new methods clear, other parts of organization influenced

7

The quality of working life

The product of our adult life is like a shell,
which protects the growth of the fruit
inside. As soon as we realise that the shell
is not of essential value, we may make use
of what we find in ourselves. However, it is
possible that one uses work and inner
strength to produce no more than an outer
shell of success, possessions and
pretensions, and then towards the end of
one's career, suddenly, one may quite
literally experience oneself as an empty,
burnt-out and rigid shell, and find one has
gained little of any value. (Herbst, 1975,
p. 440)

Historical retrospect

Work is a central aspect of many people's lives, but it is only in
recent years that the quality of the experience of work itself has
become a focus for serious study. As we indicated in chapter 2, for
a great many people the quality of working life is very poor. This
emerged clearly in a survey by Davis *et al.* (1972) of the ways in
which the content of jobs was decided upon by managers in
American industrial organizations. They concluded:

Current job design practices are consistent with the principles of rationalization or scientific management. They minimize the dependence of the organization on the individual. At the same time they minimize the contribution of the individual to the work of the organization, i.e. its production process. (Davis *et al.*, 1972, p. 80)

As a result, the authors note, managers now find they have to make considerable efforts to compensate for the demeaning nature of the jobs they have created and to seek, by various forms of propaganda, to persuade employees of their importance to the organization.

The principles described by Davis have been, and still are, widely used in developed countries of both the east and west to design industrial and clerical jobs. They have their origins in the work of F.W. Taylor who, in the first years of this century, formulated the principles of what he termed 'scientific management'. Taylor was an American engineer whose prime concern was the efficiency of men and machines. Through the subdivision of labour, the 'rationalization' of jobs into unit functions, technical streamlining of production and the strictest use of time, Taylor was able to achieve vast improvements in productivity. In his opinion, all the discretionary elements in work should be lodged with managers who, by careful administration of financial rewards, could then effectively control a workforce organized according to his principles. So economically successful was his approach that, modified and refined by later theorists and practitioners (including time-and-motion study specialists, work study engineers and ergonomists), it became the dominant and largely unquestioned orthodoxy in the design of work.

Although Taylorism has been subjected to occasional and vehement criticism from its earliest days, the search for alternative approaches to job design did not get under way until the 1960s and early 1970s when, as workers' expectations and work opportunities were fast developing, the psychological and behavioural consequences of job simplification (e.g. lack of involvement, absenteeism) began to concern employers. The work of psychologists in the previous decades and subsequently was to lay the foundations of what is now an impressive body of job-design theory, as well as a practical technology of work re-design that has been both successful and influential.

During the late 1950s and early 1960s two new theories of job design developed that were soon to capture the public imagination. One was Herzberg's 'motivator-hygiene' theory (1966), the other the theory of 'socio-technical systems'. Herzberg's theory owes a lot to Maslow's theory of motivation that we mentioned in chapter 5 (p. 78), with its insistence that 'higher order needs' would become important motives in people's lives, once their basic needs were met, an insight particularly relevant to a society beginning to enjoy a period of security and prosperity. Herzberg's theory of motivation makes this same point, but perhaps more strongly. Based on an analysis of times when people had felt exceptionally good or bad about their jobs, he suggests that people at work are motivated by two separate categories of need. One is their need to avoid pain, the other their need to 'self-actualize' (although Herzberg's use of the term is somewhat broader than Maslow's). Herzberg believes that when people's need to 'avoid pain' at work is not met they feel very dissatisfied, but the satisfaction of this need does not lead them to be satisfied with or involved in their jobs. For this to occur, their needs to self-actualize have to be met through interesting work, responsibility, achievement, advancement and similar factors. In this way, Herzberg claims, 'hygiene' factors (related to the conditions under which people do their jobs) and 'motivators' (concerned with the content of the work) each have a different kind of effect. Money, good supervisors, working conditions and security, that is the factors upon which managers, traditionally, have placed most emphasis, may make for an acceptable work environment. However, it is factors inherent in the job that transform motivation from a concern with pain avoidance to a positive involvement in achievement-oriented behaviour.

The second new approach to job design, that of socio-technical systems theory, developed from the work of Trist and others at the Tavistock Institute of Human Relations in London, to which we have referred earlier (see chapter 4). This suggested that, in designing jobs, attempts should be made to reconcile both the technological requirements and workers' social and psychological needs. In other words, jobs should be designed with a recognition that psycho-social factors both limit what is technically practicable and yet, if properly understood, allow a wider range of possible job designs than would previously have been considered. While Herzberg's approach was used primarily as a justification for enriching individual jobs, socio-technical theory indicated that groups of workers involved in collaborative work could be encouraged jointly to manage their own activities, with the discipline of their own self-management replacing regulation by machine or by supervisor.

Ideas such as these heralded a significant challenge to the prevailing orthodoxy. Many advocates of the new approaches saw them as offering potential for a worker involvement hitherto unrealized, a path both to people's personal development and to the democratization of the work place. Thus Davis and Cherns (1975), in an observation that encapsulated the pioneering spirit of the times, observed:

> A number of US and Western European organisations, some in association with University researchers, have undertaken experiments that have changed conditions and relationships and led to enhanced satisfaction, more qualified people and greater commitment at work. The problem now is to determine how these pioneering changes can be generalised, built upon and extended. (Davis and Cherns, 1975, p. 7)

In table 11, taken from Trist's (1981) account of the evolution of socio-technical theory, the differences between an orientation which seeks primarily to involve workers in their jobs and one which is designed to control them are summarized. They show why, for Trist and others, the new approaches to job design represented nothing less than a new paradigm of work organization.

However, throughout the 1960s it was not clear to all observers that the new psychological approaches to job design were as radical as their supporters claimed. Among the doubts expressed some referred to the precise formulation of the relevant theories themselves and others to the uses to which they were being put. For example, it was argued that not all workers put as much store on intrinsic benefits as the theories implied, and that individual differences were insufficiently acknowledged. It was also suggested that the general significance to workers of extrinsic factors (especially job security and remuneration) was not sufficiently emphasized. In highlighting the neglect of intrinsic factors in older approaches, the criticism was made that the new approaches allowed the pendulum to swing too far the other way.

A further criticism related to the practical implications of job

Table 11 Old and new paradigms for the design of jobs

Old paradigm	New paradigm
The technological imperative	Joint optimization
People as extensions of machines	People as complementary to machines
People as expendable spare parts	People as resources to be developed
Maximum task breakdown, simple narrow skills	Optimum task groupings, multiple broad skills
External controls (supervisors, specialist staffs, procedures)	Internal controls (self-regulating subsystems)
Tall organization chart, autocratic style	Flat organization chart, participative style
Competition, gameplaying	Collaboration, collegiality
Organization's purposes only	Members' and society's purposes also
Alienation	Commitment
Low risk-taking	Innovation

After Trist (1981).

enrichment and autonomous work group theory. The call to incorporate discretionary elements within jobs was widely recognized as helpful but, in the early days of job re-design theory, it was not altogether clear exactly what the exhortation meant in practice. It was suggested by some sociologists that the rhetoric of job-design theory sounded more impressive than the results of any re-design process actually looked. In particular, it was not clear how far the new approaches to job design challenged established management 'prerogatives' to determine and control the activities of subordinates. The feeling developed in some quarters that, as extensive re-design of work was likely to be costly, only marginal and cosmetic, changes to the content of jobs were likely to emerge from the new approaches.

A final concern should be noted to the effect that, while apparently championing the personal development of workers, what was being promoted was a new work ethic. It is not evident that changes in the 'how' of work organization will necessarily affect people's sense of personal value if the 'what' of their jobs remains unchanged. Work is a social activity, relating producers to users. Arguably, if workers have a low regard for the outcome of their work the precise mode of its arrangement will have little impact on their opportunity to 'self-actualize' through their jobs. Poor quality goods and services, harmful or undesirable products seem unlikely vehicles for people's self-fulfilment and, as we noted in chapter 5, the self-actualizing person may choose to achieve this off the job.

Now, some twenty years after the first attempts to improve the quality of working life, a number of significant developments can be recorded. Job-design theory is nowadays more precise; the relation of job re-design to organizational power structures is better appreciated; and lastly, the claims made for it are now more sensible and more innovative than previously. In the remainder of this chapter we discuss each of these points and their implications for psychological interventions in the design of work.

Developments in the theory of job re-design

The theory of job design has developed most significantly in two ways. First the consequences of impoverished work are now better understood. Karasek (1979), for example, notes how people in demanding jobs which do not allow them much opportunity to exercise discretion show a high incidence of pill-taking, absentee-ism, exhaustion and low job satisfaction. However, it would be wrong to conclude that it is members of managerial and profess-ional groups who are most at risk in their jobs from stress-related diseases. As Fletcher and Payne (1980) conclude in their review of stress research, despite popular myths to the contrary, those who suffer most stress are people of low socio-economic status doing low level work in organizations. They note that repetitive, machine-minding-type tasks appear to be particularly unpleasant and potentially harmful to health and well-being. The strain of boredom arising from underutilized abilities at work may not be noticed initially, but, persisting for months or years, it can reach chronic levels. Workers exposed to such strains who are also subject to difficulties in their lives outside work are especially at risk because their abilities to cope with complex demands have been undermined by years of stagnation in their jobs. Therefore, housing, marital or financial problems may escalate. By describing a cycle of stimulus deprivation at work, reduced ability to cope with complex problems, fewer supports, greater stressors and a greater incidence of maladaptive coping behaviours (e.g. smok-ing), Fletcher and Payne go some way in explaining the far higher incidence of stress-related illnesses and lower life expectations of those with a poor quality of working life.

Hackman and Oldham (1976) have proposed a model of the ways in which people respond to their jobs which is shown on figure 4. It suggests that, depending upon the priority that workers themselves place on opportunities for personal growth in their jobs, certain core job dimensions (autonomy, feedback, task identity etc.) lead to particular psychological states (e.g. feelings of responsibility) which, in turn, result in outcomes such as high motivation, job satisfaction and low absenteeism. This theory is more specific than Herzberg's ever was, pointing as it does to those particular dimensions in the organization of jobs likely to be related to reactions such as job interest and achievement.

Analysis of the circumstances under which semi-autonomous groups can be created in work organizations has also developed. A crucial precondition of these is the existence of a 'whole task' around which the group can be given responsibility over planning, execution and progress control of its work. The size of the group too is now recognized to be important; it should be big enough to include within it all the skills the group's task might normally

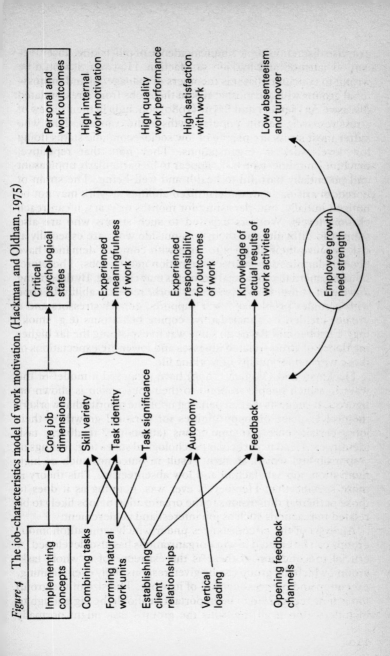

Figure 4 The job-characteristics model of work motivation. (Hackman and Oldham, 1975)

Implementing concepts

- Combining tasks
- Forming natural work units
- Establishing client relationships
- Vertical loading
- Opening feedback channels

Core job dimensions

- Skill variety
- Task identity
- Task significance
- Autonomy
- Feedback

Critical psychological states

- Experienced meaningfulness of work
- Experienced responsibility for outcomes of work
- Knowledge of actual results of work activities

Personal and work outcomes

- High internal work motivation
- High quality work performance
- High satisfaction with work
- Low absenteeism and turnover

Employee growth need strength

require, but not so big that members find it difficult to identify with the group as a unit. For group members to work well together they need to develop a degree of mutual trust and respect. Furthermore the concept of group autonomy itself has been clarified by Gulowsen's (1972) analysis of factors related to autonomy. He points out that semi-autonomous work groups vary in the amount of freedom they can be allowed, with increasing degrees of autonomy distinguished by an increasing number of areas over which the whole group exercises control. These areas are listed in figure 5. It should be noted that there are relatively few examples in the literature of work systems designed to allow groups the considerable autonomy that Gulowsen's factors indicate is possible. (Towards the highest levels of autonomy on Gulowsen's scale the group begins to look something like a sub-contracted workgroup). However, the recent fashion for introducing 'quality circles' into work organizations is an important example of the trend towards allowing worker groups greater local autonomy. Quality circles are groups of people who meet regularly to discuss issues relating to their productivity and work quality. As such, they provide more opportunity for people to become involved in, and influential over, matters relevant to their jobs and job performance than is given to many employees.

Developments in the practice of job re-design

In the practice of job re-design, over the years there has been a marked shift from relying on outside technical experts for advice on how to involve the people whose jobs are to be re-designed in

Figure 5   Stages of workgroup autonomy. (After Gulowson, 1972)

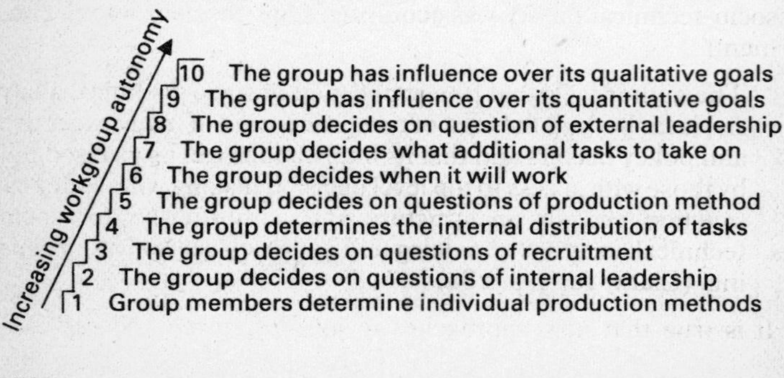

Increasing workgroup autonomy

10   The group has influence over its qualitative goals
9   The group has influence over its quantitative goals
8   The group decides on question of external leadership
7   The group decides what additional tasks to take on
6   The group decides when it will work
5   The group decides on questions of production method
4   The group determines the internal distribution of tasks
3   The group decides on questions of recruitment
2   The group decides on questions of internal leadership
1   Group members determine individual production methods

any planning and experimentation. Initially, Herzberg argued that the correct approach to re-designing jobs was to exclude the workers themselves. He claimed that by involving people in the re-design of their work, any subsequent attempts to assess the effects of the enriched jobs would be difficult. He thought that the interest generated by participation in the re-design of their jobs would have a significant, though only temporary, effect on workers' commitment and he was particularly concerned to establish the credibility of new forms of job design, especially as not all managers were easily convinced of the economic viability of his new approach. But, as we saw in the last chapter, however well intentioned they may be, imposed changes often provoke resistance and it is now recognized that it is unwise and arrogant to assume that others know best what groups and individuals like in their work.

While Herzberg's approach to job re-design today seems authoritarian, the early approach to socio-technical re-design seems jargon-laden and elitist. Following early attemps to conduct socio-technical analysis, guidelines formulated in the late 1960s (Hill, 1971) spoke of 'scanning the target system', identifying 'unit operations', discovering 'key variances' affecting work and workers, ascertaining how far these are 'controlled by the social system', examining 'social-system members' perceptions of their roles', looking at 'neighboring systems', 'boundary-crossing systems' and the 'general management system', then 're-cycling' where necessary, to culminate in job re-designing proposals. The basic ideas here are both sensible and rather simple, but the use of systems terminology in describing them serves more to obfuscate than to enlighten. There is no doubt that some social scientists were not displeased at the aura of technical complexity that socio-technical theory was acquiring. One observer was to comment:

> The author feels that [the application of socio-technical analysis] is far beyond the area of comprehension of many executives and policy makers and that its implications can be realised only by those with access to top level decision making where they can sanction changes in structure and authority ... for socio-technical analysis ... a delegated approach seems less promising. (Clark, 1975, p. 184)

It is true that new approaches to job design may necessitate a number of other changes in an organization, but the suggestion that the application of socio-technical analysis is beyond the comprehension of many executives (and also presumably of the workers) now seems little short of absurd. Reviewing a collection of detailed reports on the 'state of the art' of job re-design practices in several European countries, Elden (1979) noted how the highly diverse group of case examples he had bought together 'share at least one striking feature: employee participation in the planning and management of organization change'. He further notes the common characteristics of the most advanced examples in the collection:

- a design team [is formed] representative of (if not elected by) the employees – at the very least employees agree to a change of effort;
- employees receive some training in work redesign concepts and techniques;
- participatory search processes initiate the change effort and are not necessarily limited to the design team;
- the design team develops its own criteria and alternatives (little reliance on installing some predesigned package);
- all employees participate at least in evaluating alternatives;
- there is a high degree of participation in all phases of the redesign process (planning, developing alternatives, evaluating, etc.) which is focused and paced by the people affected (not primarily by management or change experts);
- outside experts have a shared learning role that changes over time (*from* some teaching *to* learning *with* the participants and eventually to learning *from* them).

(Elden, 1979, pp. 373–4)

Training in work-re-design approaches is an important feature of this re-design process. In the last chapter we argued that organizational development consultants set out not to change an organization themselves, but to help organizational members solve their own problems. Here too, as Elden notes, the objective of the job re-design trainer is not to tell people what to do, but to help create the conditions under which they can re-design their own jobs for themselves. Thus, the advances in job-design theory that we have illustrated can be used not only as the basis of a new technology of job design that experts can employ but also as a pool of ideas from which job holders themselves can draw in the process of re-designing their own work.

Job design and the organization

The process of job re-design in an organization does not stop when the jobs themselves have been modified. As systems theory indicates, an important change in one area of an organization can be expected to lead to significant effects elsewhere. Therefore the need for employee-training may be greatly enhanced, selection practices may need revision, new payment systems may become necessary (perhaps by increasing the salaries of workers employed in enriched jobs or by introducing a group-bonus system for a semi-autonomous group). Further, promotion opportunities may be reduced when jobs have been re-designed, as fewer supervisors and middle managers may be needed. Indeed, the conventional role of the supervisor is likely to change quite radically after a job re-design programme. As work is conventionally arranged, supervisors often need to spend a lot of time acting as progress-chasers and inspectors, but when people themselves take responsibility for their work supervisors need to act more as helpers and trouble-shooters, working with rather than directing their subordinates. Finally, it should be noted that changes such as these will not pass unnoticed elsewhere in the organization. Other people may then request new job designs or may perhaps develop misgivings about what has been happening. It should be noted that the output of people in re-designed jobs often improves, placing extra demands on the work of related sections and, in the long term, sometimes making it possible to employ fewer people.

It should be emphasized that this list of related changes is no longer than one compiled of developments implied by other, more well-accepted, organizational improvements. For example, the introduction of a new staff-appraisal system or of new budgetary or cost-control arrangements or of new services or products are all likely to require widespread supportive changes. Even so, job re-design changes do have certain features that distinguish them from many other changes designed to make organizations more effective. This is because the ideology guiding job re-design theory differs from the dominant ideology of most work organizations. Personal development and individual involvement are championed by new forms of work design. On the other hand, as we have already noted, managers in business organizations tend to be guided by the values of economy and profitability and are concerned to design work systems that, with these values in mind, are both reliable and robust. There are limits to most managers' commitment to re-designing work. If arrangements can be made for people to co-operate more, all well and good, but businesses exist to make a profit, they have to operate in an unsympathetic and competitive world and employees are hired to make this possible. Managers often point out that there are limits to the amount of control they feel they can sensibly devolve to others. This attitude is neatly summed up in the suggestion that many managers seek as much rationalization in the organization of work as is possible, but are prepared to allow only as much 'humanization' of work as is necessary.

While managers' interests in work reform have tended to be limited, trade unionists have not, in the main, adopted the humanization of work as a major objective. Many unionists would agree that job re-design would be beneficial to their members. But the traditional role of unions has been to improve or protect their members' jobs, conditions of employment and the payments they receive. Moreover, they have been able to do this by virtue of the power of collective action expressed through, often hard-won, procedures for collective bargaining. Job re-design expands employees' involvement in the day-to-day running of their jobs, but it does not, in itself, expand their control over broader issues. Questions of ownership and control are of crucial importance to trade unionists' understanding of the bargaining processes in which they are involved. The tendency in the UK for unions to adopt an adversarial stance in relation to management reflects this approach. Many have learned to mistrust reforms presented to employees by managers as 'for their own good' and heartily dislike approaches to thinking about organizations that fail to recognize conflicting interests of employees and employers. Trade unionists, therefore, emphasize the advantages of collective action by their members in defending their security and affirming their identity. In contrast, job re-design theory emphasizes the value of an individual's autonomy in his or her job and the significance of this for the development of confidence and purpose.

An illustrative case study

A number of these points are illustrated by the course of a particularly innovatory job design that one of the authors studied in Volvo's truck division (Blackler and Brown, 1980b). Volvo now has an international reputation for innovatory work in the field of work humanization, but in the late 1960s and early 1970s it had a poor reputation as an employer in Sweden, with high levels of staff absenteeism and turnover. To overcome this Volvo went to considerable lengths to change its practices and image, publicizing very widely its extensive efforts to re-design jobs. The company's new car-assembly factory at Kalmar was designed to avoid the worse excesses of mass-production technology. Outside the company, this plan captured the public's imagination and became widely cited as a pioneering example of the humanization the new approaches to job design could inspire. Within the company, the example of the Kalmar factory helped to foster an unusually innovative environment, with production engineers encouraged to question conventional production engineering wisdom and to experiment with new ideas.

In 1974, the company found that, because of buoyant customer demand, additional truck production was needed. At this time, however, its assembly lines were already working at maximum capacity, so a taskforce was set up to explore new possibilities for achieving the extra truck-production targets. An unconventional approach was developed which involved a semi-autonomous team of assembly workers assembling trucks around *static* chassis. Ever since the day when Henry Ford had employed Tayloristic principles in the assembly of his famous 'model T', static assembly of high volume vehicles had been thought to be far less effective than moving assembly lines. Yet, over a period of some months, the performance of Volvo Truck's experimental static assembly team improved dramatically. Studies within the company suggested that, theoretically, with certain technical innovations and a motivated, skilled and co-operative workgroup, substantial savings in assembly man hours (in the order of 30 per cent) could be achieved under this new method. The enthusiasm of the workers for the new procedures grew and, to the excitement of those responsible, the performance potential of the new method began to be realized. Although by 1976 the excessive demand for trucks had ended with the slackening of the world economy, the company did not shut down the experimental production unit. Senior managers were aware that, within a few years, Volvo might need to design and build a new truck-assembly factory and, following the success of the experimental assembly unit, it seemed sensible to explore further the feasibility of this new way of building trucks.

The method of static assembly is particularly interesting from a psychological point of view, maximizing as it does worker variety, learning opportunities, responsibility and involvement in a 'whole task'. Not only does it avoid the problems of task fragmentation but it makes it possible for operators to take on many extra tasks, such as checking material supplies and undertaking quality-control tasks. Accordingly, this assembly method can involve operators in many of the traditional tasks of the production engineer, necessitating important alterations in conventional patterns of management control. The work in progress on conventional vehicle-assembly lines is, of course, tightly controlled by management, whose computer aided information systems ensure that the correct components are available to the assembly workers as they are required. Static assembly methods, however, are based on a different principle, with work in progress and the pace of its completion much more under the direct control of the operators themselves.

In 1976 not all managers in the truck division were as impressed by the potential of the new assembly method as the design team had been. Various qualms were expressed. It was argued that the results of one small study could not be generalized to a large new assembly factory. Certain technical difficulties were emphasized. The assumptions, basic to the static assembly method, that people could cope and were trustworthy did not impress all managers. None the less the idea that a new plant could be built, based on the new assembly method, seemed to have a definite chance of success at this time, principally because of the significant commercial possibilities that it seemed to offer.

However, by 1979 opinion had hardened. The experimental static assembly unit was found lacking after certain changes had been introduced: the size of the assembly team had been altered, the assembly of different trucks had been tried, higher work targets had been set. Serious difficulties resulted, with the performance and morale of the operators dropping markedly. Management therefore decided not to proceed with the static assembly of trucks any further. The new truck factory was designed along more conventional lines, with the assembly of each truck divided between six teams along an assembly line. It was a system that was undoubtedly more advanced than those in comparable factories, but was far less progressive than the original static assembly indicated was possible.

There are a number of reasons why the promise of the original experimentation was lost. One feature, in particular, of the early (and successful) experimental static assembly work in the 1974–6 period had concerned senior management. At that time, once the workers had completed their allocated daily quota they were allowed the privilege of some relaxation around their work station. Management did not like this, however, and later sought to control the 'slack' by increasing work quotas which, not surprisingly, had a demoralizing effect on the assemblers. (It says much for the pervasiveness of the protestant work ethic that the response of these Swedish managers was exactly the same as that of British and American managers to workers whose bonus schemes enabled them to complete an agreed quota and then take some leisure on the job – if people are not working to capacity all the time it is inferred that the standards set are too low.) Some errors in judgement followed when the original design team was replaced by a group rather less experienced in socio-technical analysis. These included the increase in size of the assembly team and poor training when the team was asked to assemble a new truck. Later management was to acknowledge these mistakes, but to conclude that their impact confirmed the view that static assembly was not as reliable and robust a method as the conventional assembly line. Despite any potential commercial advantage that static assembly might have, the loss of management control that it necessitated was regarded as an insurmountable obstacle.

The trade unions' involvement in this case is of interest. Swedish unions have taken a more active interest in job re-design than most and, early on, made efforts to help the company's experimentation with static assembly. But, in the economic recession which began in the late 1970s, they became suspicious of new methods that could reduce jobs. Moreover, management/union relations in Sweden took a turn for the worse when the social democrats lost power and a more conservative government took office. A period of management/labour confrontation was then to begin and, in a growing climate of distrust, the unions, while not active in stopping further work on the static assembly of trucks, were not to protest as its demise.

The future for job re-design

A number of points emerge from the previous discussion. The experience of work for a great many people is very poor and constitutes a major social problem. The theory and practice of job design goes some way to identifying why this is the case and what can be done about it. Yet, important though the humanization of work undoubtedly is, there are limitations to the extent to which job re-design alone can be expected to contribute to fundamental work-place reform. Its underlying ideology differs both from the prevailing dominant values of work organizations and of trade unions, differences made more obvious in recent years as the economic recession has deepened. Consequently, there is a danger that, despite the good intentions of psychologically inspired theories of job design, the potential for the reforms that they have highlighted may remain unrealized. The question arises, therefore, of the future for psychological approaches to improving the quality of working life and, in particular, of the ways in which the adoption of such approaches can best be encouraged.

As a preliminary comment, we would stress that it is *limiting to regard job re-design itself as a primary change objective.* In chapter 6 we showed that it is a mistake for outsiders to seek to impose solutions in the interests of organizational development. The key tasks of intervention that we identified (working with people's 'felt needs', helping them to mobilize their efforts, to make operational their objectives and to institutionalize the new behaviours) are designed to highlight the unique contribution of the psychologist as a 'specialized helper' in assisting people to solve their own organizational problems. While organizational psychology points towards certain general principles concerning the circumstances under which people experience satisfying work, it is unwise to seek to promote one particular technical solution. Job re-design theory has made an important contribution to the development of approaches to improving the quality of working life and there are reasons to believe that it has pinpointed a very serious problem. However, job re-design has to be recognized as but *one* means by which people can become more self-managing and effective in their work.

A number of consequences follow from this. First, even when specific interest has been expressed by a client in work humanization it would be wrong to adopt too prescriptive an approach. To facilitate the process of self-managed organization design, one approach is to help the client develop a personal *network* of people who may have useful experience from which he or she can benefit. 'Workshops' can be arranged for managers, workers and trade unionists who have had experience with job re-design to discuss it with others who are presently considering embarking on some re-design project. Site visits may be arranged, and information exchanged about useful resources that people can draw upon. In this way the danger that job re-design knowledge may be thought to be the exclusive property of outside and remote 'experts' can be overcome. Moreover, 'packaged' solutions are likely to be avoided as, having embarked upon such a 'search' process, people are likely to be more creative in developing solutions that suit their own particular needs.

Secondly, given that, despite its importance, job re-design is not the sole means of improving people's involvement and control of their work, a *multi-level approach* to organizational reform is desirable. Many structural approaches, including traditional attempts to introduce industrial democracy, have been criticized by psychologists on the grounds that they have negligible impact on the everyday experience of employees. Electing worker directors to the boards of companies may, for example, have no effect on the working lives of the people they represent. But this does not mean that structural changes are unimportant. The economic, political, legal and technological dimensions of organizational activities and environments are such that psychologists working in organizations should not restrict their attention to personal and interpersonal issues only. They need to consider and explore the consequences of technological change, organizational hierarchies, ownership and control, and of relevant government policy and legislation in relation to psychological health and well-being.

Thirdly, psychologists should not be too preoccupied with the novelty of their own definitions of problems. People's interest in new approaches may wane and, no matter how sensible the ideas, it can be counter-productive to keep on re-emphasizing one's pet theory. If they are to have a long-term impact on the quality of working life, psychologists should develop *a sensitivity towards the prevailing concerns of others*. There are many areas where psychological objectives and the objectives of particular interest groups overlap. Managers' concern for productivity and efficiency provides scope for psychologists to make progress on matters related to the experience of work even if, as we have seen, there are

Table 12 Alternative perspectives on the diffusion of psychological approaches for improving the quality of working life

Key issues	Alternative approaches		
(1) What is to be promoted?	Particular techniques of organizing	*v.*	An appreciation of general psychological issues and a search for localized solutions to relevant problems
(2) Where should the reform attempt be focused?	At the personal and interpersonal levels only	*v.*	Intervention at the personal and interpersonal levels supported by a multi-level approach to workplace reform
(3) How should prevailing perceptions of organizational problems be regarded?	Exclusive concentration on problems highlighted by psychological theory	*v.*	Working also on those issues regarded as important by different interest groups and which are compatible with psychological priorities
(4) How should progress be evaluated?	In terms of how far predetermined change objectives are reached	*v.*	An approach to evaluation which stresses incrementalism, developing goals and process-oriented issues

limitations to what may be achieved. Trade unionists' concerns such as the health and safety of their members provide similar scope. By exploring ways in which they can work with trade unionists on such issues, psychologists can make important contributions to the re-design of work. A growing concern of managers, trade unionists and governments alike is the impact that new micro-electronic based technologies will have on work organizations. Psychologists have an important potential role to play in this matter in helping to ensure that the new technologies are used in sensible ways, to encourage greater decentralization and employee responsibility rather than facilitating more efficient centralized control.

Finally, we would observe that progress in improving the quality of work experience should be evaluated *less in terms of the achievement of specific objectives and more in terms of the development of self-managing processes*. It is, of course, helpful to know how many jobs have been restructured when assessing the significance of a company's efforts in this respect. But, given that change objectives may vary as a reform programme proceeds, targets that once seemed sensible may become less relevant. Moreover, as the major psychological objective of job re-design is the development of people's skills of self-management, specialized indicators of how successfully this aim has been achieved should be sought. People's subjective assessments of the value of their involvement in a change project, for example, would be one appropriate approach.

In table 12 we summarize these points. Job re-design theory has been one of the major success stories of applied psychology in recent years. It points to a number of important lessons for the development of an influential applied psychology of the future.

8

Problems and perspectives in organizational psychology

In recent decades increasing attention has been paid to the psychology of the worker; but this very formulation is indicative of the underlying attitude; there is a human being spending most of his lifetime at work, and what should be discussed is the industrial problem of human beings rather than the human problem of industry. (Eric Fromm, 1955, p. 181)

Developments and progress within organizational psychology

In this concluding chapter we turn to the future of applied psychology in organizations, in particular to the directions in which the theory and practice of organizational psychology might most usefully be developed. This is a difficult issue as predicting the future is a notoriously unreliable occupation! Nevertheless, we feel that there are good reasons to believe that the situation through the late 1980s and beyond will take the subject in new directions and provide it with new opportunities for contributing to practical affairs.

Ideas about the ways in which progress takes place within a

science have been transformed in recent years by Kuhn's (1962) account of *The Structure of Scientific Revolutions*. The conventional view is that scientific progress is dependent on the acquisition of new data relevant to a problem issue. Usually these data are collected by using a rigorous scientific methodology, thereby enabling people to distinguish between alternative plausible explanations of the matter at hand. On this view the expectation is that progress will occur incrementally and cumulatively as more and more knowledge is discovered. But, even within the natural sciences, the idea that progress follows the smooth path of incremental additions to knowledge has not born close scrutiny. Studies of the ways in which science has, in practice, developed, have produced accounts that are at variance with conventional, usually idealized, suggestions as to what ought to happen. While rigour in method is undoubtedly important, it would appear that progress in science does not necessarily follow a predictable path.

In his account of progress in science, Kuhn uses the term 'paradigm' to refer to an established pattern of ideas that guide people in their approach to problem-solving. When used to refer to developments in the natural sciences, Kuhn's 'paradigm' describes a state where a scientific community works within a prevailing and pervasive theoretical, methodological and ideological framework. Thus there is broad agreement between scientists as to the appropriate explanatory framework, research approaches and system of values that should guide their work. Emphasizing the importance of the community of scholars, Kuhn's view is in accord with Boring's (1952) statement that 'scientific truth is *truth by agreement*, a social kind of truth'. According to Kuhn, the most significant advances in science occur when the credibility of existing approaches and priorities (the prevailing 'paradigm') within a subject are stretched beyond acceptable limits. On this view, as inadequacies in the established patterns of ideas that have guided scientific problem-solving become exposed within the scientific community to the point of intolerability, 'paradigm shifts' occur. New approaches to theory, alternative methodologies and new priorities emerge to replace older approaches. Accordingly, the major epistemological reconstructions of a Galileo, a Newton or an Einstein come to be accepted as the basis for a new orthodoxy.

Accounts such as this make it clear that, in the normal course of events, some strain will exist within a scientific community.

Scientists will present their research data and ideas to their colleagues who will (with reference to criteria such as the knowledge they already accept, prevailing standards of rigour, acceptability and so on) form a judgement of it. Predictably, therefore, advocacy will play an important part in this process. New and unusual ideas and interpretations may appear worthless, odd or even threatening to established figures. Kuhn (1963) himself is rather disparaging on this point, quoting from Planck that 'a new scientific truth is not usually presented in a way that convinces its opponents . . . rather, they gradually die off, and a rising generation is familiarized with the truth from the start'. However even though the process may not be entirely logical, on Kuhn's analysis, periods of most rapid change and development in the natural sciences occur when a scientific community recognizes the importance of the unacceptability of conventional approaches and acknowledges the need for a new paradigm.

Combining as it does insights into the behaviour of scientific communities with an appreciation of scientific theory and method, Kuhn's account of progress in science has a certain plausibility. However, it is not at all clear that his account of paradigm shifts can be used to describe progress in the social sciences as well as it describes periods of dramatic change in the natural sciences. Psychology is notorious for the wide diversity of approaches it includes. Behaviourism, humanistic psychology, psychoanalytic approaches and ethogenics, for example, have little in common. It makes little sense to talk about one guiding pattern of ideas in the subject and more to talk about the existence of a limited number of competing paradigms. Moreover, there is the point that, as we have seen in our previous discussion of the history of organizational psychology, major developments in social science do not depend only on the scientific community becoming aware of inadequacies in the internal logic of mainstream approaches. While Kuhn's paradigm shift occurs as a result of internal tensions, factors such as emerging preoccupations with new problems and shifts in predominant values and ideologies have, as we argued earlier, been equally important in prompting new developments in organizational psychology.

Developments within organizational psychology, therefore, have to be seen in a wider context. This includes socio-economic and political factors as well as psychological ones. However, the suggestion that different paradigmatic approaches exist within the discipline is a helpful one. We have previously commented on the tentative nature of guidelines to action that is inevitably characteristic of many relevant theories in organizational psychology. Applied psychologists need to work with guides to action that must remain but approximations. They also need to resolve uncertainties about which theoretical approaches to adopt (e.g. behaviourism or humanistic psychology), what problems to concentrate on (e.g. effectiveness in organization or employee welfare) and who is to be their client. Much as natural scientists depend on their community of peers to learn (normally through exemplary expositions) how best to approach their task, so too do applied psychologists turn to their professional peers for help in resolving such issues. 'Schools of thought' thus emerge. The 'NIIP approach', for example, would have referred to the pragmatic orientation of the members of the National Institute of Industrial Psychology (see chapter 1) towards areas such as selection and training. The 'Tavistock approach' refers nowadays to an action oriented approach often (though not always) emphasizing the psychodynamics of groups and characteristically concerned to reconcile both technological and psycho-social requirements at the workplace.

At their most sophisticated such orientations can be described as 'paradigms of practice'. Referring less to the techniques of intervention that a practitioner may employ, we intend that the term 'paradigm of practice' should refer to the general class of ideas that guide his or her practice. Just as Boring could comment that scientific truth is 'truth by agreement' so it would appear that, in applied social science, common practices emerge from a developing consensus within a community of practitioners as to appropriate theoretical, methodological and ideological frameworks. Because of the importance of an established pattern of ideas to guide the practitioner, it is not uncommon within organizational psychology to find eloquent and committed advocacies of particular paradigms of practice. Indeed, the process of advocacy is in this field perhaps more evident than in some other branches of science. As we discussed in chapter 5, organizational psychologists address not only an academic audience but also a target population of managers, administrators, workers and trade unionists, whose views on appropriate approaches to organization are every bit as firmly held as are the more fully articulated theories of social scientists.

In table 13 we summarize some of the changing approaches to applying psychology that we have commented on within this book. Yet the shifts which we summarize in the table have not taken place after a period of crisis such as those Kuhn believes occur in times of major change in the natural sciences. According to his account the most significant developments in a science take place when, as the internal logic of the prevailing paradigm becomes convoluted to the point of self-contradiction, a scientific community experiences tension and dismay. But within organizational psychology (and no doubt within other areas of applied social science also) major developments have occurred for a variety of reasons. The transition from 'industrial' to 'organizational' psychology that we recorded in chapter 1, the progress of research into ageing in chapter 5, the development of 'organizational development' in chapter 6 and of research into the quality of working life in chapter 7, all occurred in large part because of the tensions arising from changing social conditions, emerging values and a growing awareness of new priority problems. Methods and theories within the subject have no doubt greatly developed as a result of internal logical considerations and are nowadays more sophisticated than previously. But important 'paradigm' shifts in the subject have not occurred because of matters of internal consistency alone.

At the time we are writing three problem areas seem likely to be particularly significant to developments in the subject within the UK and other western industrialized countries. They are (a) a period of relative or actual decline in economic performance; (b) the existence of large numbers of long-term unemployed; and (c) the widespread adoption of micro-electronic based technologies within work organizations. Such problems as these promise to change radically the field of organizational psychology, engaging practitioners in new problem areas and theorists in new concerns.

Emerging organizational problems and the future for organizational psychology

The general effects of the *period of economic decline* facing the UK are both well known and considerable. Public-service expenditure is increasingly commanding scrutiny and, long term, it seems likely that severe economies will continue to be demanded. Private sector organizations have been less uniformly affected but with

Table 13 Old and new 'paradigms of practice' within organizational psychology

Key issue	Old approach	New approach	Examples
(1) In whose interests is the organizational psychologist working?	The social scientist as a value free expert	A recognition of the importance of the values of organizational psychologists	Organization change in Shell (chapter 6)
	Human problems treated as technical problems	A recognition of the differing interests within organizations	
(2) What is the role of the organizational psychologist?	An expert analyst	A facilitator of localized activity	'Organizational development' (chapter 6)
	To search for the 'best' ways of organizing	To encourage eclecticism	
(3) How may changes best be introduced?	Consideration of particular problems only	A recognition of the interlocking nature of organizational problems	Job re-design in Volvo (chapter 7)
	An attempt for once-and-for-all change with respect to them	Incrementalism	
(4) What claims to knowledge can organizational psychologists make?	A search for 'laws' of behaviour	An emphasis on concepts, models and theories	Attempts to encourage improvements in the quality of work life (chapter 7)
	Prescription for what should be done	The need for local enquiry to determine the relevance of theory in any particular case	

manufacturing industries badly hit and, with the continuing decline of important sectors of the economy forecast and only restricted opportunities for growth elsewhere, the prospects for many are not good. The demands for cost savings and improved efficiency have raised many issues of conflict within organizations and seem likely to continue to do so in the foreseeable future.

In these circumstances a number of trends are apparent. In private sector oganizations, there has been a strengthening of the 'dominant ideology' (see chapter 3) of economic rationality. In the public sector a new ideology of 'value for money' has been imposed where, previously, concern for service or care has been paramount. This has meant that work on 'the quality of working life' is, for all except the more enlightened managers, becoming thought of as a luxury item. Concern for industrial democratization also has faded with the term 'worker involvement' replacing previous discussion about 'worker participation'. Long-term, psychological approaches to organizational effectiveness can expect a better reception than can psychological approaches to job satisfaction and participation.

While the concerns of efficiency and effectiveness are obviously of considerable social importance we are not also arguing that the need to find ways to humanize organizations is passed. We discuss below how the need for continuing attention to the design of jobs will be needed. We would also argue that the need for collaborative management styles will be an issue of lasting significance. At a time of retrenchment a greater reliance within organizations on the use of 'legitimate authority' (see chapter 4) can be predicted. The bureaucratic form of organization concentrates power in the hands of a few who can defend their authority, under the defence of its legality and economic rationality. An expert basis of authority is less likely to be used in times of continuing scarcity, as the views of one expert can be questioned by another. But, by emphasizing the prerogative to manage, the 'political' nature of decision-making in organizations that we discussed in chapter 3 can be concealed behind an idealized image of rights and reason. Although we would argue that the need for increased collaboration and devolution of powers will be great in the years to come, the consolidation of bureaucratic hierarchies seems a more likely development.

One aspect of the changing economic circumstances has been the *growth of long-term unemployment*. As the numbers of unemployed have grown it has been suggested that efforts should be made to avoid the stigmatization of people who are out of work. But even if the emphasis society normally places on the value of having a job could be reduced, it is by no means clear that the problems of the unemployed themselves would be greatly helped. Jahoda (1979) has argued that in addition to its 'manifest functions' (e.g. financial remuneration), work fulfils certain 'latent functions' in people's lives. She notes how workers can take a deeply felt pride in their work despite its sometimes trivial nature. Work, she argues, imposes a time structure on the day, ensures regular contacts with other people, links a person to goals and purposes other than his or her own, enforces activity (rather than idleness) and confers stature and identity. It is difficult to see how any other single activity can provide fulfilment on this scale. New approaches to careers (see chapter 2) and other developments such as job sharing, part-time working and the like offer partial solutions. But organizational psychologists may find it helpful to draw on a broad range of psychological theory in considering this matter. Developmental psychology has many insights into how people adjust within their life cycles. To help people cope with the problems of the transient society that we mentioned in chapter 1, it may be necessary for organizational psychologists to work with both educational and clinical psychologists to develop ideas that may influence relevant social policies and practices. Intervention in schools and in the family is likely to be more beneficial in helping people develop the skills and capacities to cope with changing social conditions than are interventions within work organizations.

Finally it should be noted that adoption of *micro-electronic based technologies* will profoundly influence organizations. The new technology promises to affect many different functions, from computer aided design, through computer aided manufacturing, quality control, warehousing, marketing, supply and purchasing. Office work will be substantially re-organized as the information revolution changes both secretarial and clerical work and transforms managerial and professional jobs. The cost of much of the new machinery based on micro-electronics puts it within the reach of most organizations and, in time, it is clear that micro-electronic systems will be widely installed in work organizations.

The new technologies can be used in a number of ways. They

can be used to facilitate a more effective development of staff. They can permit a considerable amount of decentralization of information, and mechanization of routine tasks, thereby freeing workers for more interesting tasks. But it is by no means sure that this is how they will be used. Taylor's 'scientific management' (see chapter 7) was specifically designed to take control of work away from the workers, placing it in the hands of those above them in the hierarchy. Deskilling, however, was not possible beyond a certain level. Nowadays the situation has changed and computerization promises to make possible the mechanization of highlv complex professional skills. It seems possible that rather than being used as an adjunct to human beings the new technologies will be used in ways to replace them, to employ people as mere adjuncts to the machines or to use the machines to control people's activities. (A headline in *The Engineer* of January 1980 announced that 'keeping tabs on shop-floor activity is a job for the micro-processor'.) Although a lot is now known about how changes in organizations can be introduced with the participation of those involved (see figure 3), past experience with job redesign theory (see chapter 7) suggests that a certain pessimism is in order about the likelihood that such procedures will generally be followed. The opportunities for major organizational review that the introduction of new technologies can provide will be lost, if they are adopted in a piecemeal fashion as simply the latest technological gadget available. Moreover, as our discussion of managing change suggested, if the new technologies are imposed on people, it is unlikely that they will be fully utilized. The real challenge of the new technologies to organizations is not what new hardware or software can be developed, but how behavioural considerations can be given as much priority as technological matters undoubtedly will be.

Brief though this discussion of potential problems has been, it should be clear that, while psychology has considerable relevance to developing organizational problems, it cannot solve them alone. Politicians, government officials, managers and trade unions all have their contributions to make, as do economists, sociologists and technical experts. As we emphasized at the conclusion of the last chapter (table 12), applied psychologists should not primarily seek to promote their own particular techniques but should work with compatible interest groups, guided by an appreciation of general psychological issues with an emphasis on a joint search for localized solutions, and with a multi-level strategy for organizational reform in mind.

Developments in the identity of the discipline

In chapter 5 we discussed the idea of 'giving psychology away'. In part, our conviction that psychologists should work closely with their clients on relevant problems reflects our view that to give the subject away is an important and worthwhile endeavour. Yet the role of the 'specialized helper' that we have described in this book is intended to acknowledge the limits to which psychology can be given away and to point towards the distinctive skills of the organizational psychologist in his or her helping role.

There is no doubt that non-psychologists can (and do) develop important intervention and self-management skills from their contacts with organizational psychology. Group-process sensitivity, social skills in leadership, techniques of job re-design and organizational intervention are good examples of the ways in which important aspects of the subject can (and should) be given away. However, it is not belittling the importance of such achievements to point out that, in some circumstances, it is easier to help people acquire behavioural skills than it is to equip them with rich conceptual insights into analytical theory and guiding principles. The organizational development interventions described in this book were not intended to achieve this latter objective and, in any case, most people would not be inclined to invest the time and effort needed to develop a broad knowledge of psychology. Herzberg's theory, for example (see chapter 7) while poorly regarded by psychologists nowadays, is accepted readily enough by hard-pressed managers who want no more than a general rule of thumb to help guide their approach. It is less in the actions of interventionists themselves and more in the precision and insights of the accounts that are offered of the success or failure of such actions that organizational psychologists are often most easily distinguished from the clients they have worked with.

In the light of our comments in chapter 5 about the problematic relationship between thought and action, this conclusion may seem unremarkable enough. However, it points to the suggestion that, despite their inevitable concerns with prevailing problem issues, organizational psychologists should not lose sight of the importance of strong links with their basic discipline. Knowledge of individual differences is fundamental to the methods of selection and assessment described in chapter 3, for example, and understanding of the structure and functioning of organizations considered in chapter 4 rests on basic psychological studies of roles and of social interactions within groups. Through a sound appreciation of psychological theory, organizational psychologists will not only be better equipped to help their clients help themselves but will also be well placed to contribute to theoretical developments in the field. An example of the need for this follows from our earlier discussion of the evident conflicts between different interest groups in work organizations during periods of economic decline. Organizational psychology has in the past utilized social psychological theories of group behaviour and sentient processes to illuminate such conflicts. What has been absent and may now be useful is the application of cognitive approaches to help explain communication problems between different groups. It is evident, for example, that when experts from different fields get together the modes and imagery they use for construing the world differ markedly. The ways in which some experts conceive of problems may not be immediately comprehensible to others. For mathematicians, trained to think in terms of mathematical formulae, or for engineers, trained to work with quantification and control of variances, the tentative, partial and incomplete nature of psychological knowledge often seems unsatisfactory. For their part psychologists often find it difficult to work with technologists whose thought processes are so dissimilar from their own. Yet one recurring lesson from the matters we have considered in this book is the importance of psychologists working with such experts. Study of the cognitive differences that hinder such collaboration has been neglected in recent years. Approaches from psycho-linguistics, however, could perhaps be adapted for and applied within organizational settings.

Finally we would comment that in large part the distinctive contribution that organizational psychology can make to practical affairs arises from the functions that its theories can serve. Theories can help illuminate what is happening in an organization (e.g., how group norms affect behaviour), how behaviour can be influenced (e.g., by group-training theory or the theory of organization structures) and what alternatives to present arrangements are a possibility (e.g., theory of motivation and of leadership). At its best organizational psychology draws attention to how we do and how we might live our lives. In this it can serve a liberating function, by increasing the insights people have into their own and others' behaviour and by helping them explore new action strategies.

Suggestions for further reading

Chapter 1

Sofer, C. (1972) *Organizations in Theory and Practice*, London, Heinemann.

NIIP (1970) *Occupational Psychology*, vol. 44, London, National Institute of Industrial Psychology.

Chapter 2

Argyris, C. (1975) *Personality and Organization*, New York, Harper.

Child, J. (ed.) (1973) *Man and Organization*, London, Allen & Unwin.

Meakin, D. (1976) *Man and Work*, London, Methuen.

Chapter 3

Pfeffer, J. (1981) *Power in Organizations*, Marshfield, Mass., Pitman.

Porter, L.W., Lawler, E.E. and Hackman, J.R. (1975) *Behavior in Organizations*, New York, McGraw Hill.

Salaman, G. and Thompson, T. (eds) (1973) *People and Organizations*, London, Longman for the Open University Press.

Chapter 4

Child, J. (1977) *Organization: A Guide to Problems and Practice*, London, Harper & Row.

Katz, D. and Kahn, R.L. (1978) *The Social Psychology of Organizations*, 2nd edn, New York, Wiley.

Chapter 5

Cherns, A.B. (1979) *Using the Social Sciences*, London, Routledge & Kegan Paul.

Nicholson, N. and Wall, T.D. (eds) (1982) *The Theory and Practice of Organizational Psychology*, London, Academic Press.

Chapter 6

Argyris, C. (1970) *Intervention Theory and Method*, Cambridge, Mass., Addison Wesley.

Mangham, I.L. (1978) *Interactions and Interventions in Organizations*, Chichester, Wiley.

Chapter 7

Bailey, J. (1983) *Job Design and Work Organisation: Matching People and Technology for Productivity and Employee Involvement*, London, Prentice Hall.

Cooper, C. and Mumford, E. (1979) *The Quality of Working Life in Western and Eastern Europe*, London, Associated Business Press.

Chapter 8

de Wolff, C.J., Shimmin, S. and de Montmollin, M. (1981) *Conflicts and Contradictions: Work Psychologists in Europe*, London, Academic Press.

References and author index

The numbers in square brackets are the pages on which the reference is mentioned

Aitkin, R. J. (1965) *Vaginal temperatures* ... ... [ ]

Andrewartha, H. G. and Birch, L. C. (1954) *The Distribution and Abundance of Animals*, Chicago University Press.

American Fertility and ... ...

Pavlidina, in Industry, Progress. Advances ... ... industry, Chicago, Chicago Press. [ ]

Argyris, G. (1960) *Emotions and Organization* ... ...

Argyris, G. (1962) *Interpersonal Competence and Organizational Effectiveness*, New York: Wiley. [ ]

Argyris, C. (1964) *Integrating the Individual and the Organization*, New York: Wiley. [ ]

Argyris, C. (1960) *Innovation, Research and ... ... systems*, Addison-Wesley.

Argyris, C. (1965) *Dynamics of ... ...*, Homewood, Dorsey-Irwin. [ ]

Bales, R. F. (1950) *Interaction Process Analysis*, Cambridge Mass.: Addison-Wesley. [ ]

Barnard, C. I. (1938) *The Functions of the Executive*, Cambridge, Harvard University Press. [ ]

References and name index

The numbers in italics following each entry refer to page numbers in this book.

Ackoff, R. L. (1969) 'Systems, organizations, and interdisciplinary research', in Emery, F. E. (ed.) *Systems Thinking*, Harmondsworth, Penguin. *5*

American Psychological Association Task Force on the Practice of Psychology in Industry (1971) 'Effective practice of psychology in industry', *American Psychologist*, 26(11). *11*

Argyris, C. (1957) *Personality and Organization*, New York, Harper. *26, 78*

Argyris, C. (1964) *Integrating the Individual and the Organization*, New York, Wiley. *78*

Argyris, C. (1968) 'Some unintended consequences of rigorous research', *Psychological Bulletin*, 7, 185–97. *71*

Argyris, C. (1970) *Intervention Theory and Method*, Cambridge, Mass., Addison Wesley. *96*

Argyris, C. (1976) 'Theories of action that inhibit learning', *American Psychologist*, 31, 638–54. *58*

Bales, R. F. (1951) *Interaction Process Analysis*, Cambridge, Mass., Addison Wesley. *50*

Belbin, E. (1964) *Training the Adult Worker, DSIR Problems of Progress in Industry No. 15*, London, HMSO. *74*

Belbin, E. (1979) 'Applicable psychology and some national problems', *British Journal of Psychology*, 70, 187–97. *10*

Bell, G. D. (ed.) (1967) *Organizations and Human Behavior*, Englewood Cliffs, N. J., Prentice-Hall. *2*

Bennis, W. G. and Slater, P. E. (1968) *The Temporary Society*, New York, Harper & Row. *26*

Beyer, J. M. and Trice, H. M. (1982) 'The utilisation process: conceptual framework and synthesis of empirical findings', *Administrative Science Quarterly*, 27, 591–622. *70*

Blackler, F. and Brown, C. (1980a) *Whatever Happened to Shell's New Philosophy of Management?*, London, Saxon House. *92*

Blackler, F. and Brown, C. (1980b) 'Job redesign and social change: case studies at Volvo', in Duncan, K. D., Gruneberg, M. and Wallis, D. (eds) *Changes in Working Life*, London, Wiley. *117*

Blake, R. R. and Mouton, J. S. (1964) *The Managerial Grid*, Houston, Gulf. *55*

Blau, P. M. and Schoenherr, R. A. (1971) *The Structure of Organizations*, New York, Basic Books. *36, 37*

Boring, E. G. (1952) 'The validation of scientific belief', *Proceedings of the American Philosophical Society*, 96, 535–90. *125*

Brotherton, C. (1980) 'Paradigms of selection validation: some comments in the light of British Equal Opportunities legislation', *Journal of Occupational Psychology*, 53, 73–9. *29*

Brown, L. D. (1973) 'Action research: hardboiled eggs out of eggheads and hardhats', in Green, T. B. and Ray, D. F. (eds) *Academy of Management Proceedings*, Boston, Mass., Academy of Management, *69*

Burns, T. and Stalker, G. M. (1966) *The Management of Innovation*, 2nd edn, London, Tavistock. *15, 37, 66*

Chadwick-Jones, J. K., Nicholson, N. and Brown, C. (1982) *Social Psychology of Absenteeism*, New York, Praeger. *43, 44*

Cherns, A. B. (1976) 'Behavioural science engagements: taxonomy and dynamics', *Human Relations*, 29, 905–10. *76*

Cherns, A. B. (1979) *Using the Social Sciences*, London, Routledge & Kegan Paul. *70*

Child, J. (1977) *Organization: A Guide to Problems and Practice*, London, Harper & Row. *38*

Chin, R. and Benne, K. (1969) 'General strategies for effecting changes in human systems', in Bennis, W., Benne, K. D. and Chin, W. (eds) *The Planning of Change*, 1st edn, New York, Holt, Rinehart & Winston. *95*

Clark, P. A. (1975) 'Intervention theory: matching role, focus and content', in Davis, L. E. and Cherns, A. B. (eds) *The Quality of Working Life*, vol. 1, New York, Free Press. *113*

Davidson, M. A. (1977) 'The scientific/applied debate in psychology: a contribution', *Bulletin of the British Psychological Society*, 30, 273–8. *70*

Davis, L. E., Canter, R. R. and Hoffman, J. (1972) 'Current job design criteria', in Davis, L. E. and Taylor, J. C. (eds) *Design of Jobs*, Harmondsworth, Penguin. *104, 105*

Davis, L. E. and Cherns, A. B. (1975) *The Quality of Working Life*, vol. 1, New York, Free Press. *107*

Department of Employment (1971) *Glossary of Training Terms*, London, HMSO. *32*

de Wolff, C. J., Shimmin, S. and de Montmollin, M. (1981) *Conflicts and Contradictions – Work Psychologists in Europe*, London, Academic Press. *70*

Downs, S. (1980) 'Facilitating change: two problem areas and suggestions for their solution', in Duncan, K. D., Gruneberg, M. M. and Wallis, D. (eds) *Changes in Working Life*, Chichester, John Wiley.

Dunnette, M. D. (1976) *Handbook of Industrial and Organizational Psychology*, Chicago, Rand McNally. *6, 12*

Dunnette, M. D. and Borman, W. C. (1979) 'Personnel selection and classification systems', *Annual Review of Psychology*, 30, 477–525. *8*

Dunnette, M. D., Campbell, J. and Argyris, C. (1968) 'A symposium: laboratory training', *Industrial Relations*, 8, 1–45. *97*

Elden, M. (1979) 'Concluding notes', in International Council for the Quality of Working Life *Working on the Quality of Working Life*, Leiden, Nijhoff. *114*

Emery, F. E. (ed.) (1969) *Systems Thinking*, Harmondsworth, Penguin. *4*

Fletcher, B. C. and Payne, R. L. (1980) 'Stress and work: a review and theoretical framework', *Personnel Review*, ix, 1, 19–29; ix, 2, 5–8. *110*

Fox, A. (1974) *Beyond Contract: Work, Power and Trust Relations*, London, Faber & Faber. *41, 42, 43*

French, J. and Raven, B. (1967) 'The basis of social power', in Cartwright, D. and Zander, A. (eds) *Group Dynamics Research and Theory*, New York, Harper & Row. *57*

Fromm, E. (1955) *The Sane Society*, New York, Harper. *124*

Goffman, E. (1959) *The Presentation of Self in Everyday Life*, Garden City, N.Y., Doubleday. *86*

Gulowsen, J. (1972) 'A measure of work group autonomy', in Davis, L. E. and Taylor, J. C. (eds) *Design of Jobs*, Harmondsworth, Penguin. *112*

Hackman, J. R. and Oldham, G. R. (1976) 'Motivation through the design of work', *Organizational Behaviour and Human Performance*, 16, 250–79. *110, 111*

Handy, C. B. (1976) *Understanding Organizations*, Harmondsworth, Penguin. *23, 49*

Harrison, R. (1970) 'Choosing the depth of organizational intervention', *Journal of Applied Behavioural Science*, 6, 181–202. *98*

Harrison, R. (1972) 'Understanding your organization's character', *Harvard Business Review*, May/June, 119–28. *88, 90*

Hearn, J. (1981) 'Crisis, taboos and careers guidance', *British Journal of Guidance and Counselling*, 9, 12–23. *25*

Herbst, P. (1975) 'The product of work is people', in Davis, L. E. and Cherns, A. B. (eds) *The Quality of Working Life*, vol. 1, New York, Free Press. *104*

Herzberg, F. (1966) *Work and the Nature of Man*, Cleveland, World. *78*, *106*

Hill, P. (1971) *Towards a New Philosophy of Management*, London, Gower. *92, 113*

Hinrichs, J. R. (1976) 'Personnel training', in Dunnette, M. D. (ed.) *Handbook of Industrial and Organizational Psychology*, Chicago, Rand McNally. *32, 34*

Holdsworth, R. (1983) 'Personnel selection', in Williams, A. P. O. (ed.) *Using Personnel Research*, London, Gower Press. *30*

Jahoda, M. (1979) 'The impact of unemployment in the 1930s and 1970s', *Bulletin of the British Psychological Society*, 32, 309–14. *131*

Janis, I. L. (1972) *Victims of Group-Think*, Boston, Houghton Mifflin. *51*, *52*

Kahn, R. L., Wolfe, D. M., Quinn, R. P., Snoeck, J. D. and Rosenthal, R. A. (1964) *Organizational Stress: Studies in Role Conflict and Ambiguity*, New York, Wiley. *23*

Karasek, R. A. (1979) 'Job demands, job decision, latitude and mental strain: implications for job redesign', *Administrative Science Quarterly*, 24, 285–308. *109*

Katz, D. and Kahn, R. L. (1978) *The Social Psychology of Organizations*, 2nd edn, New York, Wiley. *5*

Keenan, T. (1980) 'Stress and the professional engineer', in Cooper, C. A. and Marshall, J. (eds) *White-Collar and Professional Stress*, Chichester, Wiley. *23, 24*

Kelman, H. C. (1965) 'Manipulation of human behaviour: an ethical dilemma for the social scientist', *Journal of Social Issues*, 21, 31–46. *81*, *82*

Klapp, O. (1969) *Collective Search for Identity*, New York, Holt, Rinehart & Winston. *26*

Klein, L. (1976) *A Social Scientist in Industry*, London, Gower Press. *11*

Kuhn, T. S. (1962) *The Structure of Scientific Revolutions*, Chicago, Chicago University Press. *125*

Kuhn, T. S. (1963) 'The function of dogma in scientific research', in Crombie, A. C. (ed.) *Scientific Change*, London, Heinemann. *126*

Landy, F. J. and Trumbo, D. A. (1980) *Psychology of Work Behavior*, rev. edn, Homewood, Ill., Dorsey Press. *34*

Law, B. (1981) 'Community interaction: a "mid-range" focus for theories of career development in young adults', *British Journal of Guidance and Counselling*, 9, 142–58. *21, 22*

Levine, N. and Cooper, C. (1976) 'T groups – twenty years on, a prophecy', *Human Relations*, 29, 1–23. *97*

Levinson, H. (1972) *Organizational Diagnosis*, Cambridge, Mass., Harvard University Press. *17*

Lewin, K. (1947) 'Frontiers in group dynamics: concept, method and reality in social science', *Human Relations*, 1, 5–13. *46*

Lewin, K. (1967) *Field Theory in Social Science*, London, Tavistock. *68*

Likert, R. (1961) *New Patterns of Management*, New York, McGraw Hill. *55*

Lupton, T. (1966) *Management and the Social Sciences*, London, Hutchinson. *6*

Lytle, W. O. (1975) 'A smart camel may refuse the last straw: a case study of obstacles to job and organization design in a new manufacturing operation', in Davis, L. E. and Cherns, A. B. (eds) *The Quality of Working Life*, vol. 2, New York, Free Press. *77*

Maier, N. R. F. (1970) *Problem Solving and Creativity in Individuals and Groups*, Belmont, Calif., Brooks Cole. *58*

McGregor, D. (1960) *The Human Side of Enterprise*, New York, McGraw Hill. *78*

Mangham, I. L. (1978) *Interactions and Interventions in Organizations*, Chichester, Wiley. *87*

Mangham, I. L. (1980) 'The limits of planned change', in Trebesch, K. (ed.) *Organizational Development in Europe*, Berne, Haupt. *84*

Marris, P. (1974) *Loss and Change*, London, Routledge & Kegan Paul. *84*

Maslow, A. H. (1954) *Motivation and Personality*, New York, Harper. *78*

Merton, R. K., Reader, G. G. and Kendall, P. L. (eds) (1957) *The Student Physician*, Cambridge, Mass., Harvard University Press. *27*

Miller, E. J. and Rice, A. K. (1967) *Systems of Organization*, London, Tavistock. *4*

Miller, G. A. (1969) 'Psychology as a means of promoting human welfare', *American Psychologist*, 24, 1063–75. *78*

Nicholson, N. and Wall, T. D. (eds) (1982) *The Theory and Practice of Organizational Psychology*, London, Academic Press. *5*

Palm, G. (1977) *The Flight from Work*, Cambridge, Cambridge University Press. *18, 26*

Patrick, J. (1980) 'Comments on Section II', in Duncan, K. D., Gruneberg, M. M. and Wallis, D. (eds) *Changes in Working Life*, Chichester, Wiley. *76*

Perrow, C. (1970) *Organizational Analysis: A Sociological View*, London, Tavistock. *13*

Pettigrew, A. M. (1976) 'Towards a political theory of organizational intervention', *Human Relations*, 28, 191–208. *59*

Pfeffer, J. (1981) *Power in Organizations*, Marshfield, Mass., Pitman. *41*

Porter, L. W., Lawler, E. E. and Hackman, J. R. (1975) *Behavior in Organizations*, New York, McGraw Hill. *29, 33*

Roberts, K. (1977) 'The entry into employment: an approach towards a general theory', in Williams, W. M. (ed.) *Occupational Choice*, London, George Allen & Unwin. *19*

Robertson, I. and Downs, S. (1979) 'Learning and the prediction of performance: development of trainability testing in the United Kingdom', *Journal of Applied Psychology*, 64, 42–50. *30*

Roethlisberger, F. J. and Dickson, W. G. (1939) *Management and the Worker*, Cambridge, Mass., Harvard University Press. *9*

Schein, E. H. (1965) *Organizational Psychology*, 1st edn, Englewood Cliffs, N. J., Prentice Hall. *35*

Schein, E. H. (1980) *Organizational Psychology*, 3rd edn, Englewood Cliffs, N.J., Prentice Hall. *2, 20, 26, 36, 46, 47, 78*

Shamir, B. (1978) 'Between bureaucracy and hospitality: some organizational characteristics of hotels', *Journal of Management Studies*, 15, 285–307. *66*

Shepherd, A. and Duncan, K. D. (1980) 'Analysing a complex planning task', in Duncan, K. D., Gruneberg, M. M. and Wallis, D. (eds) *Changes in Working Life*, Chichester, Wiley. *76*

Sprott, W. J. H. (1958) *Human Groups*, Harmondsworth, Penguin. *46*

Stinchcombe, A. (1969) 'Social structure and the invention of organizational forms' in Burns, T. (ed.) *Industrial Man*, Harmondsworth, Penguin. *67*

Super, D. E. and Bohn, M. J. (1971) *Occupational Psychology*, London, Tavistock. *19, 20*

Susman, G. I. and Evered, R. D. (1978) 'An assessment of the scientific merits of action research', *Administrative Science Quarterly*, 23, 582–603. *71*

Sykes, A. J. M. (1962) 'The effects of a supervisory training course in changing supervisors' perceptions and expectations of the role of management', *Human Relations*, XV, 227–43. *35*

Thomason, G. A. (1981) *A Textbook of Personnel Management*, 4th edn, London, Institute of Personnel Management. *33*

Thompson, J. D. (1973) 'Society's frontiers for organizing activities', *Public Administration Review*, 33–4 (July/August), 327–35. *1, 3*

Trist, E. (1981) 'The evolution of socio-technical systems', in Van de Ven, A. and Joyce, W. (eds) *Perspectives on Organizational Design and Behaviour. 63, 107, 108*

van Maanen, J. (1979) 'Preface for seminar on reclaiming qualitative methods for organizational research', *Administrative Science Quarterly*, 24, 520–26. *45*

van Strien, P. J. (1978) 'Paradigms in organizational research and practice', *Journal of Occupational Psychology*, 51, 291–300. *82*

Vernon, H. M. (1948) 'An autobiography', *Occupational Psychology*, XXII (2), 73–82. *7*

Vroom, V. H. (1964) *Work and Motivation*, New York, Wiley. *19*

Vroom, V. H. (1976) 'Can leaders learn to lead?', *Organizational Dynamics*, Winter, 17–28. *56*

Wallis, D. (1971) 'Reflections on turning professional', *Occupational Psychology*, 45, 91–8. *77*

Warr, P. B. (ed.) (1978) *Psychology at Work*, Harmondsworth, Penguin. *70*

Warren, A. (1978) *Trainability Tests: A Practitioner's Guide*, Research Paper SL2, Industrial Training Research Unit Ltd., Cambridge, England. *31*

Watson, G. (1976) 'Resistance to change', in Bennis, W. G., Benne, K. D. and Chin, R. (eds) *The Planning of Change*, 2nd edn, New York, Holt, Rinehart & Winston. *84*

Weber, M. (1947) *The Theory of Social and Economic Organization*, New York, Free Press. *60*

Welford, A. T. (1976) 'Thirty years of psychological research on age and work', *Journal of Occupational Psychology*, 49, 129–38. *72, 75*

Wilensky, H. A. (1960) 'Work, careers and social integration', *Social Science Journal*, 12, 543–60. *25*

Williams, A. and Woodward, S. (1983) 'Attitude surveys', in Williams, A. P. O. (ed.) *Using Personnel Research*, London, Gower Press. *75*

Wyatt, S. (1950) 'An autobiography', *Occupational Psychology*, XXIV (2), 65–74. *7, 8*

Subject index

The references section of this book serves as a name index. Names are included in this index only where there is no corresponding literature citation; in most cases these are the names of historical personages.

absenteeism, 43–4, 63, 105, 110, 117
action research, 10–11, 70–1, 77
action, theory of, 58–9
ageing, 72–5
assessment centres, 31–2
attitude surveys, 8, 75–6, 99
authority, 38, 57, 130 (*see also* leadership, politics, power)
autonomous workgroups, see socio-technical systems theory

bereavement, 84–6
brainwashing, 48–9
bureaucracies, 60–2, 64–5, 130, 180

careers, 18–26, 33; guidance, 34
change: group reactions to, 86–8; individual reactions to, 84–6;

organizations and, 88–90; participation within, 96, 101–3, 114–15, 120; planned organization change strategies, 95–103; Shell case, 91–5; stereotypes of, 84
Civil Service Selection Board, 9–10
collective bargaining, 43
cultures, organizational, 88–90

division of labour, 18, 24, 41, 46, 104–9
dominant ideologies, 39–40
dramaturgical analogy, 86–8

Employment and Training Act, 33
employment: contract of, 16; entry into, 19 (*see also* occupational choice)

ergonomics, 10
expectations, 38, 54, 60, 76, 105

Ford, Henry, 117

groups, 46–7; conformity within,
    51–2; cohesion of, 50;
    psychological functions of, 47–50;
    T groups, 96–7, 100
'groupthink', 51–2, 58

Hawthorne studies, 9, 46
Health of Munition Workers
    Committee, 7
'human assets accounting', 27
'human resources', 9, 27–8

identity, 47–9 (see also self-concept)
inclusion, partial, 16
induction crisis, 15–16
industrial psychology, 6–11
Industrial Health Research Board, 7,
    8
Industrial Training Act, 33

job design, history of, 104–9
job re-design: future for, 120–3, 130;
    management attitudes to, 115–16,
    119; modern practices of, 112–14;
    organizational development and,
    99; trade unions and, 116, 119,
    123; theoretical developments
    within, 109–14; Volvo case,
    117–19

labour turnover, 16
leadership: bases for, 57; contingency
    model of, 56–7; importance of, 53;
    myths, 52–7; organizational politics
    and, 59–60; personality traits and,
    53–4; styles, 54–6, 58, 62, 64, 130
learning theory, 34

Mayo, Elton, 46
micro-electronic based technologies,
    123, 131–2
motivation, 43; job characteristics
    model, 110–11; motivator-hygiene
    theory, 106–13
Myers, C. S., 7, 8

National Institute of Industrial
    Psychology, 7, 8, 127
needs, 106; affiliation, 47; hierarchy
    of, 78–9
norms, 47–52, 86

occupational choice, 13, 14, 18,
    19–21
opportunity-structure theory, 21, 22
organic structures, 37, 64–5, 66–7
organizations: defined, 2–3; as open
    systems, 4–6, 85–90; influence of,
    1–2, 13–14; mechanistic and
    organic structures, 60–6
organization culture, 88–90
organization structure, 37, 60;
    bureaucracies, 60–2; comparative
    structures, 63–6
organizational development, 98–101
organizational psychology:
    applicability of, 7–11, 70–5, 133;
    developments within, 124–8,
    132–5; future for, 128–33; history
    of, 6–11; professional issues within,
    11, 80–2; roles for, 76–9, 81

paradigms, 124–6; of practice,
    127–9
performance control strategies, 36–8,
    80–2
personnel selection, 8, 38;
    discrimination within, 30; methods
    of, 29–32
Planck, M., 126
politics, in organizations, 38–41,
    59–60
power, 18, 38–41, 88, 89, 130 (see also
    performance and control strategies)
psychological contract, 16–18

quality circles, 112
quality of working life, 104–23

recruitment, 28–32
role, 3; change and, 86–90; of
    psychologists, 76–7; self and,
    21–41; social, 49, 52; stress, 21–4

scientist/practitioner debate, 68–71,
    81

selection, 8; discrimination within, 30; methods of, 29–32
self-actualization, 78–9, 106
self-concept, 20–6
sensitivity training, 96–7, 100
Shell UK, case study, 91–5
socio-technical systems theory, 63–6, 91–4, 106–9, 110, 112, 114
stress, 21–4, 110
systems theory, 4–6, 88–90

Tavistock Clinic, 10
Tavistock Institute of Human Relations, 10, 63, 91, 106, 127
Taylor, F. W., 105, 132

'Theory X', 'Theory Y', 78
trainability testing, 30–1
training, 11, 28, 29, 114; 'activity learning', 74; defined, 32–3; methods of, 34–46

unemployment, 130–1

Volvo, case study, 117–19

War Office Selection Board, 9
Weber, Max, 60
work, 24–6; ageing and, 72–5; low and high discretion, 41–4, 116; meaning of, 131; orientations to, 16